Now is the
season

Now is the season

LAURA FAIRE

NEW HOLLAND

contents

introduction

It seems like an exceptionally long journey has been undertaken to find the simplest solution - the solution that has never left us, that lives in the underlying rhythms of the earth in all our cultures. Seasonal food is simply that: food that is grown and consumed within its natural season, sharing its flavour if the soil is good and the methods of care are organic and loving. It's not rocket science - just a skill that got forgotten with the wonders of chemicals, airfreight and the demands of a consumerist society.

This doesn't mean that food export and import is bad; just that fresh produce available locally in its season is the ultimate. There are exotic foods that entire nations rely on that still need to be moved internationally: for some it's milk; for others it's dates, pistachios or bananas. However, plums in midwinter seem pointless; and foreign oranges consumed out of season are tasteless and banal.

Seasonal produce is the small but flavour-filled spring leaves of basil, the power-packed dill, the joy of the first summer tomato. And it's not just cooking - it's growing, scouring markets, and loving everything you put in your mouth with consciousness and care.

My journey with food started with a mother who cooks like a magician. Then, at fourteen (I'd lied about my age), I spent a summer washing dishes in a kitchen in Russell in the Bay of Islands, New Zealand. I returned every summer after that and began working the junior sections of the kitchen. From the first day I was allowed to ladle out a bowl of soup, I got the buzz of working with food. I was the kid who turned up to prepare 20kg of kumara (sweet potato) unpaid. Much later, after some training and experience, I became a chef, with all the million hours, cuts and burns, and joys of service under pressure.

The most important thing I have learned as a chef is that you can't make great food with rubbish ingredients. It was a natural progression to begin growing my own ingredients, and it has added a dimension and level of understanding to my cooking that I am forever grateful for. I believe strongly that seasonal, natural and wholefood ingredients are the key to good living and great taste. My garden is organic and I choose to purchase organic ingredients. I believe that the flavour is superior, the methods more sustainable and I prefer to enjoy food free from insecticides and pesticides. From a few pots on a patio to a fully fledged vegetable garden, growing your own food will always be rewarding. It is also fraught with lessons: it has slowly taught me patience and has increased my respect and love for good honest food.

Today I stand in a crowd of cooks, gardeners and food writers who have been banging the seasonal drum since the 1970s. I hope that the small ting of my triangle reaches the ears and hearts of others on their own journey to authenticity and the love of food.

7

winter

Winter is tricky, swinging from crisp nights
to misleadingly clear days. It draws slowly colder
and darker until finally afternoons are enveloped
in looming darkness and expectant rain-clouds.
Boots hold mud-clods after work in the garden;
comic woollen hats become outdoor attire.
The winter garden hides flavour underground
and in hardy bitter leaves. It makes us labour
for our supper. Winter demands comfort, warmth
and masses of flavour.

a winter menu

WARMING THE COCKLES

· Parsnip & Almond Soup with Spice Oil
· Thyme Baked Red Onions
· Steamed Cavolo Nero with Butter Sauce & Parmesan
· Celeriac & Roasted Garlic Purée
· Pan-roasted Chicken with Dates & Lemons
· Rhubarb & Apple Vanilla Sponge Cobbler

busy in the winter garden

TIME TO PLANT

- asparagus crowns
- basil (inside only)
- beetroot
- berry canes
- broad beans
- cabbage
- cape gooseberries
- dill
- garlic (shortest day)
- leeks
- lettuce
- mustard greens
- onions (shortest day)
- peas (inside)
- radishes
- shallots
  (from shortest day)
- snow peas/mangetout
- spinach
- spring onions
- sorrel
- globe artichokes
- new potatoes

TIME TO HARVEST

- Jerusalem artichokes
- avocados
- cavolo nero
- kale
- broccoli
- cauliflower
- Florence fennel
- kohlrabi
- sweet potatos
- leeks
- onions
- parsnip
- shallots
- silverbeet (Swiss chard)
- spinach
- Brussels sprouts
- squash
- swede
- turnip
- celeriac

TIME TO TEND

- feed fruit trees
- cover compost heap
- fork through worm
  castings
- sterilise seed growing
  trays
- plant and dig in green
  manure crops
- collect seaweed
  for compost
- start new compost teas
- prepare runner bean beds
- construct pea frames
- check all stakes,
  fastenings and nets
- break in and feed new
  ground with compost
- feed asparagus with
  seaweed tea

Fennel, Cardamom & Preserved Lemon Soup

A simple, fragrant, flavour-filled chicken soup to stimulate the appetite and replenish the soul.

2 tablespoons cold-pressed olive oil
2 cloves garlic, chopped
2 sticks celery, sliced
1 small onion, sliced
1 large bulb fennel, sliced
2 preserved lemons (page 42), rind only
4 cardamom pods, bruised
500ml homemade chicken stock
½ cup natural yoghurt

Heat the olive oil in a soup pan.

Add chopped garlic, celery, onion, fennel, preserved lemon rind and cardamom pods.

Cover and cook gently for 10–15 minutes, stirring occasionally, until fragrant.

Add the chicken stock and bring to the boil. Simmer for 2–3 minutes, then remove from the heat and take out the cardamom pods.

Allow the soup to cool slightly before blending in the yoghurt using a stick blender.

Takes 20 minutes
Serves 4

FENNEL | *There are two types of fennel. The fennel bulb is known as Florence fennel to differentiate it from the tall, beautiful herb that grows wild in the north of New Zealand and that gives fennel seeds. Seedlings need to be planted out in midsummer while still very small. Plant fennel in a bed in partial shade and keep well watered as, if it gets too dry, it will bolt and go to seed.*

Parsnip & Almond Soup with Spice Oil

This soup is thick and soothing, and makes a filling winter lunch. The cream and almond meal are enough of a nod to protein to provide a lasting feeling of soothing fullness.

1 tablespoon cold-pressed olive oil
1 small onion, chopped
1 stick celery, chopped
3 large parsnips, chopped
1 small potato, peeled and chopped
1 bunch parsley, stalks only
1½ cups vegetable stock
1 cup cream
70g ground blanched or natural almonds
white pepper and mineral or sea salt
spice oil to serve (page 150)

Heat the olive oil in a large, heavy-bottomed pot and slowly cook the vegetables with the lid on for 10 minutes until soft but not brown.

Add the vegetable stock and bring to the boil. Simmer until the parsnips are tender.

Blend or mash until smooth, mix in the cream and almonds and bring to the boil.

Taste and season with white pepper and mineral or sea salt.

Serve with a slick of hot spice oil.

Takes 25-30 minutes
Serves 4

Note: To make just enough spice oil to garnish this dish, use 2 tablespoons cold-pressed avocado oil, ½ teaspoon cumin, 1 teaspoon coriander, 1 teaspoon fennel, ½ teaspoon turmeric and sea salt.

PARSNIPS | *Plant parsnips in late spring or early summer directly into the ground as they don't like to be moved. Sow plenty of seed, as it doesn't germinate easily. Thin if necessary in late autumn once the top leaves are well established.*

Parsnip & Almond Soup with Spice Oil

Celery, Cavolo Nero & Baby Leek Gratin

A creamy and comforting yet very grown up version of cauliflower cheese, this side looks lovely served in a long dish.

½ bunch celery, quartered lengthwise

8 stems cavolo nero (black cabbage),
curly kale or silverbeet (Swiss chard),
stems removed

6 whole baby leeks, trimmed,
or 1 small leek quartered lengthwise

1 tablespoon butter

1 tablespoon stoneground flour

¾ cup milk

1 pinch each mineral salt and white pepper

1 pinch freshly grated nutmeg

¼ cup grated parmesan

¼ cup fresh breadcrumbs or panko crumbs

1 tablespoon butter, extra

Preheat oven to 180°C.

Wash the vegetables thoroughly and pat dry. Place in a rectangular ovenproof dish.

In a small saucepan melt the butter and add the flour. Cook for 2 minutes, stirring, until it is a lovely golden colour. Do not allow to brown. Remove from the heat and, using a fork, slowly whisk in the milk. Return to the pan and simmer, stirring, for 3 minutes or until thick. Season the white sauce with mineral salt, white pepper and a grate of fresh nutmeg.

Pour the sauce over the prepared vegetables.

Top with combined parmesan and breadcrumbs, and dot with the extra butter.

Cover with foil and cook for 30 minutes, then remove the foil and continue to cook for another 10 minutes (or brown quickly under a hot grill).

Takes 50 minutes
Serves 4-6

CELERY | *Plant celery seedlings out in spring or summer in trenches and keep well watered. Wrap the plants in paper or plastic if you like the stems pale; or leave if you prefer your celery dark and fully flavoured. Allow a plant or two to go to seed and collect the seed to use in cheese scones.*

Steamed Cavolo Nero with Butter Sauce & Parmesan

This stately looking cabbage appreciates delicate treatment: a simple sauce and a sprinkle of parmesan shows it off at its best. Always remove the central stalk as it is tough and fibrous.

16 stems cavolo nero (black cabbage)
1 cup vegetable stock (page 150)
sea or mineral salt
50g chilled butter, cut into cubes
1 squeeze lemon juice (about ½ teaspoon)
white pepper and mineral or sea salt
¼ cup finely grated parmesan

Remove the central stalks from the cavolo nero and stack the leaves in four bundles of four. Fasten each bundle with cooking string.

Bring the vegetable stock to the boil in a large, deep-sided pan with a large enough steamer basket to spread the cavolo nero out evenly. Place the steamer basket on top with the cavolo nero inside, and sprinkle with salt. Steam for 10–15 minutes. Remove and keep warm.

Keep the remaining stock simmering gently. Quickly whisk in the butter cubes, one or two at a time, to create a thin sauce. Add the lemon juice and pepper and salt to taste.

Roll the steamed cavolo nero bundles in the sauce, snip off the kitchen string and pour the sauce over. Sprinkle with grated parmesan.

Takes 15 minutes
Serves 4

CAVOLO NERO | *Cavolo nero is a brassica and a member of the cabbage family (it means 'black cabbage' in Italian). Cavolo nero grows into funny-looking mini trees. Pick the leaves from the centre. Grow in rotation with other brassicas.*

Wilted Savoy Cabbage with Cumin Butter

Wide ribbons of squeaky Savoy cabbage steamed until vibrant green, with frothy spiced butter – this side makes a delicious supper with a few cooked potatoes and a melty local cheese. White cabbage is good, but Savoy is somehow better.

½ small Savoy cabbage
1 tablespoon mineral salt
½ cup water
1 teaspoon cumin seeds
50g butter
juice of ½ lemon

Slice the cabbage into 3cm strips and wash thoroughly, toss with salt and leave to rest in a colander for 10–20 minutes. Rinse.

Bring the water to the boil in a large saucepan, add the cabbage and cook for 5 minutes, stirring until wilted.

In a small frying pan, toast the cumin seeds until they begin to pop and release their fragrance. Remove from the heat and add the butter, allowing it to melt.

Pour the cumin butter over the hot cabbage and toss with a little lemon juice.

Takes 25 minutes
Serves 4

CABBAGE | *There is a cabbage for every season, as they have a wide soil temperature range for growth (between 5°C and 18°C), but the darkest ones like winter best. For a winter supply, plant out with plenty of space in autumn. Yellow-painted stakes smeared with Vaseline help to keep away white butterflies, and interplanting with nasturtiums and spring onions is also thought to be helpful. Keep well watered for good tight heads.*

Celeriac & Roasted Garlic Purée

The method for this recipe is quite convoluted – but it is truly worth it! Based on a recipe by Auguste Escoffier (founding chef of Ritz hotels and chef at the Savoy), this purée is stunning with dark meats or deep-sea fish. It is vital that a stock of excellent quality is used. If using a store-bought stock, dilute it by half with water and check carefully before adding salt.

1 garlic bulb
1 teaspoon cold-pressed extra virgin olive oil
3 celeriac bulbs (total 600g), peeled and sliced
50g butter
1 large potato (200g), peeled and sliced
1 cup vegetable stock (page 150)
2 tablespoons cream
sea salt or mineral salt
white pepper, ground

Preheat the oven to 200°C.

Cut and remove the top fifth from the garlic bulb to expose the cloves. Pour olive oil over the garlic bulb and wrap in foil. Roast in the oven for 45 minutes.

Boil the celeriac in heavily salted water for 10 minutes. Drain.

Melt the butter in a clean saucepan and add the blanched celeriac and potato slices. Cover with the vegetable stock and simmer for 20 minutes, until the liquid has mostly evaporated. Turn off the heat.

When the garlic is roasted, squeeze the cloves into the pan with the cooked celeriac and potato. Add the cream and push the mixture through a sieve, then season with salt and ground white pepper. Serve with an extra slick of olive oil.

Takes 45 minutes
Serves 4-6

Note: *Can be made up to 3 days in advance; reheat just before serving.*

CELERIAC | *Plant seedlings out in spring or summer as you would for celery. It takes a long time for the root to swell, and the plants need a lot of watering. Interplant celeriac with celery in a slightly shady spot to help keep them moist.*

Roasted Winter Carrots with Tahini Dressing

Winter carrots are not as sweet as summer ones. Roasting brings out their hidden sweetness, and the tahini dressing complements their winter starchiness.

6 large winter carrots
2 tablespoons olive oil
3 tablespoons maple syrup
½ teaspoon salt
1 tablespoon tahini
1 tablespoon lemon juice
2 tablespoons boiling water
2 teaspoons olive oil
1 pinch salt
toasted sesame seeds
dried chilli flakes

Preheat the oven to 200°C.

Scrub the carrots, slice off the tops and tails and cut lengthwise into sixths.

Mix together the olive oil, maple syrup and salt, and coat the prepared carrots before spreading them out on 2 baking trays.

Bake for 25–30 minutes, turning and basting with leftover glaze until caramelised and sticky.

Thin the tahini with the lemon juice before whisking in the boiling water, olive oil and salt. Drizzle the tahini dressing over the carrots, then add a sprinkle of sesame seeds and chilli flakes.

Takes 25-30 minutes
Serves 4

WINTER CARROTS | *Winter carrots should be large. They are the ones left in the garden, covered in straw, from the final summer planting. They will keep better there than in the fridge, ready to use when needed.*

Thyme Baked Red Onions

Place these onions in the roasting pan when roasting a bird on a rack in the oven. The juices from the bird drip over the onions and add succulent flavour.

4 small red onions, topped, tailed and halved
¼ cup olive oil
2 tablespoons balsamic vinegar
50g softened butter
4 teaspoons fresh thyme leaves
sea salt or mineral salt and coarsely ground black pepper

Preheat the oven to 200°C.

Place the onions cut-side down in a baking dish and pour over the olive oil and balsamic vinegar. Bake for 20 minutes.

Turn each onion carefully and smear the cut side with the softened butter. Sprinkle with thyme, salt and pepper.

Bake for a further 10–15 minutes.

Takes 30-35 minutes
Serves 4

RED ONION | *The red onion is well suited to long storage if harvested correctly in midsummer. Winter onions serve as a two-way reminder – they bring to mind the warmth of the summer when they were pulled from the ground; and they remind us to plant more onions as the shortest day approaches.*

Thyme Baked Red Onions

Grilled Aromatic Herbed Fish

Aromatic herbs are the stock in trade of winter flavourings: they complement any meat, and also the heartier deep-sea fish like hapuku or groper.

800g firm-fleshed white fish
1 teaspoon finely chopped rosemary
1 teaspoon finely chopped thyme leaves
2 teaspoons finely chopped marjoram
1 garlic clove, crushed
2 tablespoons lemon juice
1 tablespoon olive oil
1 teaspoon salt
1 generous pinch white pepper

Preheat the oven to 160°C.

Wash and pat dry the fish and cut into 6cm lengths.

Mix together the rest of the ingredients and pile onto the fish pieces. Allow to rest while heating the grill or griddle pan to its highest setting.

Grill the fish for 2 minutes on each side or until it has a little colour. Transfer to the oven for 5–10 minutes.

Takes 20 minutes
Serves 4

LINE-CAUGHT FISH | *When buying fish look for 'Line-caught'. This term is appearing now on menus and refers to the method of fishing. The best way to tell in the fish shop is to look for fish with intact scales. Fish that is declared line-caught has been caught on a fishing line rather than using the ecologically damaging methods of benthic or pelagic trawling.*

Sausage & Fennel Pie

400g rough puff pastry (page 152)
6 pork sausages (approx 700g)
100g thick-cut smoked bacon, diced
1 large fennel bulb, sliced
1 small onion, sliced
1 tablespoon wholegrain mustard
1 teaspoon mineral salt and ½ teaspoon white pepper
2 tablespoons butter
2 tablespoons flour
1 cup milk
2 egg yolks

Preheat the oven to 180°C.

Grease and line a 20cm diameter, 5cm deep springform cake pan or pie dish with pastry and reserve a 22cm round of pastry for the top.

Brown the sausages and bacon in a large frying pan until the sausages are cooked enough to hold their shape when cut. Remove from the pan and slice the sausages into thick rounds.

Add the fennel, onion, wholegrain mustard, salt and pepper to the pan and cook gently for 20 minutes in the fat from the sausages. Remove and set aside.

Melt the butter in the same pan to ensure all the flavours left on the bottom are caught in the sauce, and add the flour. Cook for 1–2 minutes, then remove from the heat and stir in the milk. Return to the heat and stir constantly until very thick.

Combine the sausages, bacon, cooked vegetables and white sauce in a bowl with one of the egg yolks, spoon the mixture into the prepared pastry case and cover with the pastry round. Brush the top with the remaining egg yolk, then cut a small hole in the centre to allow steam to escape. Bake for 30 minutes.

Allow the pie to rest for 10 minutes before cutting.

Takes 1½ hours
Serves 6

Note: If using store-bought pastry, look for pastry made with butter and without additives.

Sausage & Fennel Pie

Crayfish Risotto

Risotto is part of an Italian peasant supper, so in true Italian style this dish delivers the glory of one crayfish (lobster) to four people helping to spread the cost of the crayfish a little further.

1 whole crayfish (lobster)
4 cups water (reserved from poaching)
1 carrot
1 onion
2 sticks celery
6 peppercorns
1 bay leaf
1 tablespoon cold-pressed olive oil
1 onion, diced
1 clove garlic, crushed
1 stick celery, diced
salt
1 cup arborio rice
50g butter, cubed
¼ cup fresh flat-leaf parsley leaves, chopped
1 tablespoon red wine vinegar

Bring a large pot of water to the boil, drop in the crayfish, and cook for 5 minutes. Remove and reserve 4 cups of water. The crayfish will not be fully cooked at this point – merely set and easier to handle.

Cut away the head and legs from the tail and roughly chop. Pick out the flesh from these sections and reserve. Cut the tail in half and scoop out the flesh in one piece from each half.

Place all the pieces of shell and inedible-looking bits back in the large pot with the reserved 4 cups of water, and add the carrot, onion, celery, peppercorns and bay leaf. Simmer for 20 minutes and then strain. Reserve the crayfish stock and keep it warm to make the risotto.

Heat the olive oil in a deep-sided frying pan and add the onion, garlic and celery, season with salt and cook gently for 10 minutes until clear.

Add the rice and turn up the heat to toast for about 3 minutes, stirring constantly, before ladling in the stock in batches. Stir until each batch of stock is absorbed. Fold through the reserved flesh from the legs, the butter cubes, chopped parsley and red wine vinegar.

Slice the tail meat thickly and lay it on top of the risotto, cover with a lid and allow to warm through for 5 minutes before serving.

Takes 1 hour
Serves 4

KILLING CRAYFISH | *It can be easier to ask your fishmonger to kill the crayfish than to deal to it yourself; however, a swift twist with the point of a sharp knife between the head and the shell will achieve a quick result.*

Crayfish Risotto

Pan-roasted Chicken with Dates & Lemons

Making the effort to select a bird from a farm with animal welfare credentials can be as simple as chatting to the local butcher. You may have to pay more for a happy bird, but it makes up for it in flavour.

1 chicken
¼ cup cold-pressed olive oil
mineral salt and coarsely ground black pepper
8 medjool dates, stones removed
1 lemon, cut into 8 wedges
2 cinnamon sticks
2 small bunches thyme
1 bay leaf
½ cup apple juice

Preheat the oven to 200°C.

Wash and pat dry the chicken before rubbing all over, outside and inside, with olive oil, salt and pepper.

Place 4 dates, 4 lemon wedges, the cinnamon sticks and 1 bunch of thyme inside the cavity.

Use kitchen string to tie together the legs and loop the string around the bird, tucking the bay leaf and second bunch of thyme tightly underneath.

Place the bird in a casserole dish and add the remaining dates, lemon wedges and the apple juice. Cover with a lid or with baking paper and bake for 40 minutes.

Remove the lid and cook for another 10–20 minutes or until a leg slips easily from its socket or the juices run clear.

Remove the chicken from the casserole dish and keep warm on a serving platter.

Remove the lemon wedges from the dish. Cut off and discard the lemon rind, and scrape the lemon flesh back into the dish. Process the pan juices into a rich sauce using a stick blender.

Takes 1½ hours
A chicken larger than 1.3kg will serve 4

Note: Tying the bird with string helps to keep its shape and makes the dish look pretty. It takes time and love to grow a beautiful organic chicken, so a little time and effort at the kitchen end is worth it.

Pan-roasted Chicken with Dates & Lemons

Braised Shoulder of Lamb with Jerusalem Artichokes & Kale

Jerusalem artichokes are the essence of winter. When roasted, a sweetened slightly tough skin gives way to a smooth purée that has been trapped inside, a little like roasted garlic. In a casserole or braised dish like this, Jerusalem artichokes harbour a starchy sweetness that is more satisfying than a potato - like an effortless, tasty dumpling.

1kg diced lamb shoulder
¼ cup stoneground flour
2 teaspoons mineral salt and 1 teaspoon ground black pepper
2-3 tablespoons cold-pressed peanut oil
1 onion, cut into 6 wedges
1 carrot, cut into thick chunks
6 cloves garlic, bruised
1 whole lemon, cut into 6 wedges
1 big stick of rosemary
400g Jerusalem artichokes
½ cup water
150g kale leaves, stalks removed

Preheat the oven to 160°C.

Toss the cubed lamb in combined flour, salt and pepper.

Heat the oil in a large casserole dish and fry the lamb cubes in batches until brown.

Return all the meat to the pan and add the onion, carrot, garlic cloves, lemon wedges, rosemary, Jerusalem artichokes and water. Cover with a lid and cook in the oven for 2 hours, stirring once or twice.

Add the kale to the casserole dish and loosely stir through. Return to the oven for another 20 minutes until the kale has wilted and is a deep green.

Takes 2½ hours
Serves 6

Note: Cavolo nero can be substituted for the kale with the same cooking time; however, if using silverbeet (chard) or spinach, cook for only a further 10 minutes.

JERUSALEM ARTICHOKES | *Plant*
Jerusalem artichokes anywhere there is sun, way back in spring. After the tall sunflower-like flowers have been enjoyed, these nuggety little tubers are ready for the winter table. Only dig up what you need; the rest will keep better in the ground.

Orange & Barley Osso Bucco

Osso bucco is really all about the marrow in the centre of the bone. Authentically this dish should be made with sliced veal shank; however beef shank or shin will work fine. The bone adds plenty of flavour to this slow-cooked dish – but even cubed stewing beef will still be delicious, if no osso bucco can be found.

2kg osso bucco (veal shank or beef shin with bone)
½ cup flour
1 tablespoon mineral salt and 2 teaspoons freshly ground black pepper
1 tablespoon cold-pressed peanut oil
4 oranges
1 cup beef stock
2 tablespoons tomato purée
½ cup barley
1 onion, sliced
1 celery stick, sliced
400g passata (page 110) or whole peeled tomatoes, puréed
3 branches thyme
2 bay leaves
6 peppercorns

Preheat the oven to 160°C.

Gently wash and dry the osso bucco and trim off any excess fat before coating in the combined flour, salt and pepper.

Heat the oil in a pan and brown the meat on both sides, being careful not to let it burn. Remove the meat from the pan and set aside.

Use a potato peeler to cut thin strips of zest from 1 orange, before juicing all 4 oranges.

Mix together the orange juice, beef stock and tomato purée and add to the pan. Return to the heat and use a wooden spoon to scrape the pan to incorporate the flavour of the meat into the simmering liquid.

Place the osso bucco, the deglazed pan liquid and all the remaining ingredients in a large roasting dish, cover with foil and cook for 3 hours, then remove the foil and turn the meat in the liquid before returning to the oven for a final 20 minutes.

Takes 3½ hours
Serves 4

Braised Creamy Rabbit Pappardelle

The rabbit, stock and homemade pasta can be prepared a day in advance if necessary; simply cook the pasta and make the creamy sauce on the day, before serving.

1.5kg whole rabbit, skinned and gutted, with kidneys
1 small onion, chopped
1 carrot, chopped
1 clove garlic
½ a lemon
1 small bunch thyme
2 small bay leaves
6 peppercorns
1 tablespoon butter
1 tablespoon rice flour
½ cup cream
½ cup of the rabbit poaching stock
400-500g homemade pappardelle (page 154)

Poach the rabbit by placing it in a large pot with the onion, carrot, garlic, lemon, thyme, bay leaves and peppercorns. Cover with water and bring to the boil, then simmer for 30 minutes. Remove the rabbit and strain the stock. Return the stock to the pan and simmer to reduce for 20 minutes while the rabbit cools. Reserve half a cup of stock for the sauce and freeze the remainder for later use.

Remove the rabbit flesh from the bones and discard the bones.

In a saucepan, melt the butter and add the flour. Cook for 2–3 minutes until golden. Remove from the heat and whisk in the cream and the reserved rabbit stock. Return to the heat and stir until thick.

Boil the fresh pasta for 3–4 minutes in ample salted water, then drain.

Add the rabbit meat and heat through. Stir the creamy rabbit sauce through the cooked pasta and serve.

Takes 1 hour 20 minutes
Serves 4-6

Note: Serve with some winter mustard greens from the garden as a spicy winter salad.

Blackened Molasses & Grapefruit Duck Breasts

This marinade works well with 2 small whole wild ducks - simply marinate for at least 1 hour or overnight before roasting in a scorching hot oven (around 220°C) for 20-25 minutes. Delicious served as a winter meal with a spoonful of creamy garlic polenta and freshly steamed greens.

4 duck breasts (around 450-500g)
4 tablespoons organic unsulphured molasses
juice of 1 grapefruit
1 tablespoon tamari or soy sauce
2 teaspoons coarsely ground black pepper
mineral salt

Trim the excess fat from the duck breasts. (The duck fat can be slowly melted in a heavy-bottomed saucepan, stored in the fridge and reused for the most delicious roast potatoes.) Score the fat on each duck breast three times, down to the flesh.

Combine the molasses, grapefruit juice, tamari and black pepper, pour over the duck breasts and rub into the score marks. Cover and marinate for 1 hour. Discard the marinade.

Heat a heavy deep-sided frying pan until smoking. Place the duck breasts skin-side down in the pan and reduce the heat to low. Cook for 6–8 minutes to render the fat. Remove from the pan and drain off most of the duck fat.

Return the heat to high and add the duck breasts back into the hot pan, skin-side up. Cook on the second side for 3–4 minutes. Remove to a warm plate, sprinkle with salt and cover with foil and leave to rest for 5 minutes before serving.

Takes 1 hour 15 minutess
Serves 4

Note: Farmed duck breasts are rich, due to the fat under the skin. This is why the cooking time on the skin side is longer.

WILD DUCK | *Thankfully, having three brothers and lots of friends keen on hunting, there is always someone around who has indulged in the manly shooting ritual. Many duck hunters are desperate for someone to cook their booty so ask around - you'll probably know one too.*

Blackened Molasses & Grapefruit Duck Breasts

Grapefruit Marmalade Crème Brûlées

Surprisingly easy, these crème brûlées are a great mix of sweet, tart and creamy, perfect for a midwinter dessert. This recipe is best made a day in advance.

1 vanilla pod
300ml cream
4 egg yolks
1 tablespoon sugar
¼ cup grapefruit marmalade (page 40)
4 tablespoons caster sugar

Preheat the oven to 160°C.

Cut the vanilla pod in half lengthwise and run a knife along the cut sides to scrape out the seeds. Add the seeds and the pod to a saucepan with the cream.

Heat the cream until small bubbles form around the outside, but do not boil. Remove from the heat and leave to infuse.

Beat the egg yolks with the sugar until pale and thick. Once the mixture is thick, beat in 2 tablespoons of the marmalade followed by the warm cream. Strain through a sieve.

Divide the remaining marmalade between 4 ovenproof ramekins and place them in a deep-sided roasting pan. Pour the strained custard into the ramekins.

Place the roasting pan in the oven and use a jug to fill the pan with enough water to come halfway up the sides of the ramekins.

Cook for 15–20 minutes until a thick skin has formed on the custards. Remove gently from the oven, being careful not to spill the hot water or break the skins. To be safe, turn the oven off and leave the door open to cool for a while before removing.

Refrigerate for at least 4 hours or overnight to allow them to set.

Before serving, sprinkle each brûlée with caster sugar and spritz with water before firing with a brûlée torch or placing under an extremely hot grill to melt the sugar.

Takes 30 minutes, plus chilling time
Serves 4

Note: If using the grill method, it helps to place the brûlées in a roasting dish filled with ice to prevent the custard from getting too hot.

Grapefruit Marmalade Crème Brûlées

Rhubarb & Apple Vanilla Sponge Cobbler

The key here is to thoroughly cream the butter and sugar until it is the consistency of clotted cream. Once that is achieved, the topping will be outrageously good.

4 cups fresh rhubarb and apple, chopped
50g or 2 tablespoons unsalted butter, softened
½ cup sugar
1 egg
1 cup stoneground flour
1 teaspoon cream of tartar
(or 3 teaspoons lemon juice)
1 pinch mineral or sea salt
1 teaspoon baking soda
1 tablespoon milk
1 teaspoon vanilla extract
cream to serve

Preheat the oven to 180°C.

Fill an ovenproof dish with fruit.

Using an electric mixer, cream together the butter and sugar until pale and the sugar is dissolved. Beat in the egg.

Sift the flour, cream of tartar and salt into a bowl.

Combine the baking soda, milk and vanilla extract in a small bowl or jug.

Fold together the dry ingredients, the creamed mixture and the combined liquids and spoon over the prepared fruit.

Bake for 30–35 minutes until the sponge is puffed up and golden brown.

Serve with whipped cream, if desired.

Takes 40-45 minutes
Serves 4-6

Note: If substituting lemon juice for cream of tartar then add with the other liquid ingredients.

RHUBARB | *Rhubarb is best harvested from its second year if the plant is to be vibrant and long-producing. Check for winter flower heads that will need to be removed while harvesting. Lots and lots of seaweed solution diluted as a foliar spray will keep rhubarb plants lovely and healthy.*

Rhubarb & Apple Vanilla Sponge Cobbler

Five-Spice Roasted Apple Crumble

4¼ cups fresh apple, peeled, cored and sliced (or use poached or canned apples)
juice of ½ a lemon
25g butter
2 tablespoons sugar
75g butter, softened
¼ cup plain flour, sifted
1 tablespoon dark brown soft sugar
1 cup organic rolled oats
¼ cup ground almonds
½ teaspoon five-spice
1 pinch mineral salt

Preheat the oven to 250°C.

Place the sliced apple in a roasting pan, squeeze the lemon juice over, dot with butter and sprinkle with cane sugar. Roast for 10 minutes while making the crumble topping.

Rub together the second measure of butter, flour, dark brown sugar, oats, almonds, spice and salt.

Fill an ovenproof serving dish with roasted apple pulp.

Spread the crumble topping over the fruit, reduce the temperature to 180°C and bake in the oven for 20–25 minutes until piping hot and golden brown.

Takes 20-25 minutes
Serves 4-6

Note: To bottle apples for quick and easy crumbles all year round, see Bottled Cinnamon Apples, page 45.

Poached Tamarillos in Vanilla Custard

1 vanilla pod
2 cups cream (500ml)
4 egg yolks
½ cup sugar
8 tamarillos
4 tablespoons toasted coconut chips or long thread coconut

Split the vanilla pod in half and scrape out the seeds, and place with the cream in a heavy-bottomed saucepan. Heat the cream until small bubbles start to appear around the edge, but do not boil. Remove from the heat and leave to rest and infuse for a good 10 minutes.

Whisk together the egg yolks and sugar until pale, light and fluffy.

Remove the vanilla pod from the cream and whisk the cream into the egg yolk mixture.

Put the custard in a clean heavy-bottomed saucepan and place back on the heat. Stir continuously until thick – do not let the custard boil, as this will cause it to separate. Set the pan aside in a warm place while poaching the tamarillos.

Bring a large saucepan of water to the boil. Cut a cross in the bottom of each tamarillo before dropping into the boiling water. Simmer the tamarillos for 10 minutes before removing and plunging into iced water until cool enough to peel.

Serve with the warm custard and a sprinkle of the toasted coconut.

Takes 25 minutes
Serves 4

Note: If the custard separates it can sometimes be saved by quickly changing it to a cold pan and whisking in 3 or 4 ice cubes.

TAMARILLOS | *I killed my first tamarillo tree because I didn't stake it strongly when I planted it. I also moved house, transplanted and overwatered it. Tamarillos will grow quite tall if they have a firm stake and plenty of sun.*

Poached Tamarillos in Vanilla Custard

Tarts' Tart

Old-fashioned grapefruit is a glorious thing: large yellow orbs hang like baubles on the tree from mid to late winter. Not having the space for one myself, the grapefruit in this recipe is 'borrowed' from the grounds of the brothel down the road.

20cm round sweet shortcrust pastry case (page 153), baked blind in a fluted tart dish
4 eggs
1 egg yolk
175g caster sugar
150ml cream
1 grapefruit, zest and juice

Preheat the oven to 150°C.

Beat the eggs, yolk and caster sugar together with a wooden spoon and then strain through a sieve.

Stir in the cream and grapefruit zest and juice; the mixture will thicken at this point.

Pour into the prepared tart case and bake for 50 minutes or until nearly set: it will have a skin, but will maintain a good wobble.

Leave to cool slightly, and remove the tart from the pan when cool enough to handle but not totally cold. Cool completely before cutting.

Takes 1 hour, plus chilling time
Makes 1 x 20cm tart (serves 8)

BORROWED FRUIT | *'Foraging' fruit is one of my bad habits. If I see a lovely specimen and no one is around, well . . . you understand. On the other hand, asking first is highly advisable – and can lead to new friends. I keep in mind streets that have good fruit trees; there is a particular street nearby that is lined with grapefruit trees and, when the fruit is hanging over the street, has had a few late night visits from me!*

Tarts' Tart

Grapefruit Marmalade

A spoonful of marmalade will cheer up any pudding, lift the spirits of a humble piece of toast, brighten up a chicken gravy and soothe the soul on a work-weary afternoon. Technically this is a jelly marmalade, lovely and clear and packed full of flavour. The recipe makes 2 jars but it is easily doubled if more is required.

2kg grapefruit (1.2kg flesh)
½ teaspoon citric acid
2 litres water
3 cups sugar
¼ teaspoon mineral salt
2 pieces of muslin: 1 x 5cm square,
1 x 20cm square
kitchen string
1 large stainless steel, copper or
enamel saucepan

Place the grapefruit in the kitchen sink and pour boiling water over the top, before giving them a good scrub and a rinse. Dry off with a clean kitchen cloth.

Using a potato peeler or sharp knife remove the peel from half of the grapefruit, taking care to remove any pith from each strip of peel. Slice finely and tie up in the smaller muslin cloth.

Place the muslin bundle in a small saucepan and cover with water. Boil until the peel is soft (about an hour). When this is finished, set the peel aside and add any remaining water to the preserving pan.

Slice off as much of the white pith and peel as possible from the remaining fruit before roughly chopping the grapefruit flesh and adding it to the preserving pan with water to make up to 2 litres of water and the citric acid. Simmer for an hour and a half.

Place a large sieve over a large bowl, line the sieve with the larger piece of muslin and strain the grapefruit pulp through it. Tie the muslin and pulp into a bundle and suspend over the bowl to catch the liquid. A kitchen tap is good for this: place the bowl in the sink beneath. Alternatively leave the bundle to rest in the sieve over the bowl. Leave overnight.

Discard the fruit pulp and measure the liquid – there should be around 6 cups. Add the liquid back into the preserving pan with the sugar and reserved peel (remove or add 1–2 tablespoons of sugar if there is more or less liquid than stated).

Bring to the boil, stirring until the sugar dissolves. Boil rapidly until a drop on a saucer wrinkles when tilted, or until a sugar thermometer reads between 104°C and 107°C.

Remove any scum by skimming with a metal spoon before pouring the marmalade into warm sterilised jars and seal. Label when cool.

Takes 2½ hours over 2 days
Makes 4 x 250ml jars

Rose-scented Quince Paste

Once a common fruit in the home orchard, the quince later fell from fashion. However, it has been revived by a global craze for tapas, as the other half of manchego and membrillo. This old English family recipe for quince paste is the gemstone of any modern winter cheeseboard.

4 large quinces, peeled and cored
2 litres water
3 tablespoons rosewater
1 cup caster sugar
1 x 20cm square of muslin

Chop the quinces into small cubes. Simmer in the water with a lid on for 30 minutes, until soft.

Add the rosewater and sugar and continue to simmer until thick. Test for thickness by dropping a spoonful of paste on a saucer and tilting the saucer to see if the jam will run; when it wrinkles, it's ready. Stand a sieve lined with muslin over a bowl.

Fill the sink with hot water and place the bowl in the water. Pour in the cooked quince. Tie the muslin with the pulp into a bundle and hang it from the kitchen tap so it drips into the bowl. (The water will keep the bowl warm and prevent the paste from setting in the bowl.)

Pour the liquid into a 30cm x 20cm greaseproof-lined slice pan and leave to set.

Cut into large squares and wrap in waxed paper. Store in airtight containers in the pantry until required.

Takes 2 hours
Makes 20 squares

QUINCE | *Quince trees like a hot dry climate and need a long warm autumn to ripen the fruit. However, they will tolerate frost and low temperatures through the winter. They are pollinated by bees, so can be grown as a single tree. Pick the fruit when it is golden yellow and has a perfume of quince when held to the nose.*

Ikaroa Lemon Cordial

I have a friend who makes a ton of this cordial every year. It runs out as soon as the summer hordes arrive - it disappears into gin and tonics, or jugs of ice and wild mint.

4 big lumpy-skinned lemons
3 cups sugar
1 litre filtered water
2 teaspoons tartaric acid

Use a potato peeler to peel off any lemon peel that isn't too gnarled. Remove any remaining white pith from the peel and slice finely.

Squeeze the lemons and strain the juice. Put the juice in a pot with the sliced lemon peel, sugar, water and tartaric acid. Simmer for 15 minutes.

Wash and dry a glass bottle and sterilise it by placing in a 150°C oven for 10 minutes. Leave the sterilised bottle and the cordial to cool before pouring the cordial into the bottle.

Takes 20 minutes
Makes 1.5 litres

LUMPY LEMONS | *Lemons that look all lumpy and gnarled often conceal juice-laden flesh. Gardening has taught me not to reject the funny-looking fruit. In fact, if buying lemons, pass on the really smooth, slightly sticky fruit – it has been waxed, so its rind is best avoided.*

Lemon Curd

3 lemons, juice and zest
¾ cup sugar
6 egg yolks
1 tablespoon honey
200g chilled butter, cubed

Pulse together the lemon zest and sugar in a blender.

Combine all ingredients in a medium saucepan.

Over a medium heat stir continuously until the butter has melted and the curd has thickened. Do not boil.

Pour into sterilised jars and leave to set. Cover and keep in the fridge.

Takes 10 minutes
Makes 2 cups

Preserved Lemons

1.5kg lemons
500g sea salt or rock mineral salt
2 bay leaves
1 cinnamon stick, broken in half
1 tablespoon coriander seeds
500g extra lemons

Place the lemons in the sink, pour boiling water over and give them a good scrub.

Make deep crosses in the lemons from the tips almost to the blossom end (where they were attached to the tree), as though cutting into wedges.

Stuff each lemon with as much salt as possible – at least a tablespoon.

Pack the lemons tightly into a sterile jar with the bay leaf, cinnamon stick and coriander seeds. Press down with a wooden spoon and leave overnight.

The next day, much of the juice will have come out of the lemons and the lemons in the jar won't be as tightly packed or covered with lemon juice.

Prepare the remaining lemons as previously and add to the jars until each jar is full.

Store in a cool dark place for at least 1 month before using.

Takes 1 hour over 2 days
Makes 2 x 1-litre jars or 4 x 500ml jars

Notes: Scrubbing the lemons in boiling water helps to remove any waxes that have been applied to commercially grown lemons.

As only the rind of the preserved lemon is used, organic, spray-free and wax-free lemons are the best ones for preserving.

Iodised table salt can leave an odd aftertaste so is best avoided in preserving.

Preserved Lemons

Bottled Cinnamon Apples

2kg cooking apples
1 bowl of water
2 lemons, juice only
500g sugar
1.5 litres water
4 cinnamon sticks
6 cardamom pods
1 star anise

Prepare 2 x 1-litre capacity bottling jars by washing in hot soapy water and placing in a roasting dish in a cold oven. Turn the oven on and bring up to 150°C. Keep the jars in the oven until ready to use.

Peel and core the apples and slice thickly. Drop the prepared fruit into the bowl of water with the lemon juice added to prevent discolouring.

Dissolve the sugar in the measured water in a saucepan large enough to fit the prepared apples. Add the spices and the fruit to the hot syrup and bring to the boil.

Simmer for 10–15 minutes until soft (this will vary depending on the variety of apple). Remove from the poaching liquid.

Handling the hot jars carefully, stand the jars in a roasting pan, pack with the apple slices to 3cm from the top of the jar. Pour the syrup over until it overflows, and seal the jars. Stand where they are until cool before rinsing the outside of the jars and storing.

Takes 30 minutes
Makes 8-10 cups

APPLE TREES | *Apple trees needn't take up lots of space. They can be espaliered against walls – and can be bought already trained (although they are a bit more expensive). I have an espaliered apple tree that grows along the fence of my chicken run: it bears little apples in late spring that grow and grow into juicy red orbs for late autumn and winter.*

Orange Zest & Cinnamon Tisane

A tisane is a combination of herbs or spices steeped in water to make a drink – often medicinal. In winter I love the warming flavours of cinnamon and the refreshing taste of orange combined in this tisane.

2 cinnamon sticks, roughly crushed
4 strips orange peel, pith removed (use organic, spray-free and wax-free fruit)
1 tablespoon honey
500ml boiling water

Place the cinnamon sticks, orange peel and honey in a teapot and pour the boiling water over.

Wrap the teapot in a teatowel or tea cosy to keep warm, and leave to steep for 10 minutes before serving.

Takes 12 minutes
Makes 2 cups

Orange Zest & Cinnamon Tisane

spring

Spring is a tease; it has come-hither eyes, laden with promise. A traveller in a desert, the cook is beckoned with fresh green shoots but little substance. Spring is lean and filled with suggestion: a well-prepared store cupboard nearly empty; empty seed beds nearly full. Spring is hope, and waiting. The cook and the gardener stand ready at spring's whim for a mock summer day or steeled against winter's return, appreciating the pared-back lines of garden beds and dishes still hearty but with hints of vibrant spring greens.

a spring menu

GREEN HARVEST LUNCH

- Green Garlic & Almond Pork Terrine
- Sorrel Pesto
- Line-caught Fish Roasted in Chive, Parsley & Pink Peppercorn Butter
- Orange-scented Prawn Tortellini
- Baby Cos Leaf Caesar Salad
- Rose Fool
- Tangelo & Mint Tisane

busy in the spring garden

TIME TO PLANT

- asparagus crowns
- aubergine plants
- sow basil seed (indoors)
- beans when ground reaches 16°C
- berries
- beetroot
- cabbage
- capsicum
- carrots
- chives
- coriander
- courgettes
- cucumber
- fennel (herb)
- gherkins
- globe artichokes
- leeks
- lettuce
- oregano
- parsley
- parsnips
- peas
- potatoes
- pumpkin
- radishes
- rock melon
- shallots
- spring onions
- sunflowers
- sweetcorn
- sow tomato seed (indoors)

TIME TO HARVEST

- asparagus
- broad beans
- spinach
- globe artichokes
- new potatoes
- fennel
- Florence fennel (bulb)
- dill
- leeks
- radishes
- snow peas/mangetout
- sorrel
- tangelos
- navel oranges

TIME TO TEND

- check bird coverings on summer fruiting oranges such as Valencia
- sow seeds into prepared seedling trays
- tie back emerging berry canes
- start sowing seed indoors
- get planting

Baby Cos Leaf Caesar Salad

1 ciabatta roll (or the inside of ¼ of a ciabatta loaf), torn into pieces

2 tablespoons cold-pressed olive oil

1 pinch mineral salt and 1 teaspoon ground black pepper

3 heads baby cos lettuce, leaves washed and torn

4 rashers thick streaky bacon, cooked and chopped

¼ cup finely grated parmesan

1 egg, boiled and chopped

2 anchovies, chopped

¼ cup Caesar salad dressing (page 150)

Preheat the oven to 200°C.

Make croûtons by tossing the torn ciabatta in the olive oil, salt and pepper and baking for 10 minutes or until golden.

Combine all the salad ingredients, including the cooled croûtons, and toss in liberal amounts of dressing just before serving.

Takes 25 minutes
Serves 4

Spring Vegetable, Chicken & Lima Bean Soup

Spring chills and storms still create a need for a good hearty soup. Serve this soup with a croûton on top that is laden with Salsa Verde with Orange (page 78), to make it outrageously filling and extra delicious.

½ cup lima beans, soaked overnight

4 tablespoons cold-pressed olive oil

1 carrot, diced

1 onion, sliced

2 sticks celery, diced

2 teaspoons mineral salt and 1 teaspoon coarsely ground black pepper

4-5 cups water

1 tablespoon malt vinegar

4 chicken tenderloins, cut into thirds (or shredded leftover chicken)

50g salami, diced

2 stalks silverbeet (Swiss chard), stems removed, cut into thick strips

2 dark outer leaves Savoy cabbage, cut into thick strips

1 tablespoon fresh dill, chopped

Soak the lima beans the night before. Heat the oil in a large saucepan and sauté the carrot, onion and celery. Season liberally.

Add the measured water, lima beans and malt vinegar, bring up to the boil and simmer for 20 minutes before adding the chicken and salami. Simmer for another 20 minutes.

Add the silverbeet and cabbage and simmer until soft but still vibrant green. Stir through the dill before serving.

Takes 1 hour, plus soaking time
Serves 4-6

Steamed Artichokes with Hot Butter Dressing

This dressing is heavy on the chervil instead of tarragon, making it a more delicate version of the béarnaise sauce. It will equally rock a seared fish fillet or a handful of prawns.

2 lemons
1 bowl of water
8 small globe artichokes
1 lemon, sliced

Hot Butter Dressing
1 shallot, finely chopped
¼ cup white wine vinegar
1 small stalk of French tarragon
100g chilled butter, cubed
½ teaspoon mineral salt and
a pinch of white pepper
1 large bunch of chervil, chopped
(about ¼ cup)

Squeeze the juice of the lemons into a large bowl and top up with water.

Use a small sharp knife to slice off the stalks and tough outer leaves of the artichokes, cut them in half, use a spoon to dig out the prickly 'choke' and drop the hearts into the bowl of lemon water.

In a saucepan with a steamer basket, bring 1–2 cups of heavily salted water to the boil with the lemon slices. Place the artichokes in the steamer basket and steam, covered, for 20 minutes while making the hot butter dressing.

For the dressing, place the shallot, vinegar and stalk of tarragon in a small saucepan and bring to a rolling boil. Keep boiling until the vinegar has reduced by half. Strain and discard the shallot and tarragon.

Put a little water in a saucepan and bring to the boil. Place the reduced vinegar in a bowl and place the bowl over the saucepan. Use a whisk to beat in the butter cubes, two at a time. Keep whisking until a thick sauce is formed. Quickly stir in the salt, pepper and chervil. Keep the sauce warm until ready to serve with the artichokes.

Takes 20 minutes
Serves 4

GLOBE ARTICHOKES | *Not really for the smaller garden, these plants are large and take a long time to produce. However they are structurally stunning and have a bright blue flower that will attract bees.*

Asparagus & Ricotta Tart with Caraway Pastry

8-10 spears of asparagus, halved lengthwise, then cut in half
250g fresh firm ricotta
zest and juice of ½ a lemon
1 tablespoon fresh dill, chopped
2 teaspoons cold-pressed olive oil
½ teaspoon mineral salt
1 teaspoon cracked black pepper
400g caraway pastry (page 152)

To garnish
2 teaspoons fresh lemon zest
1 or 2 fresh dill tips
1 tablespoon cold-pressed olive oil

Preheat the oven to 180°C.

Blanch the asparagus by cooking briefly in boiling salted water.

Combine the ricotta, lemon zest and juice, dill, olive oil, salt and pepper.

Roll out the pastry into a large round shape about 0.5cm thick.

Place the ricotta mixture in the centre of the pastry round and top with the asparagus. Gently draw in the edges to nearly cover the filling ingredients, leaving a saucer-sized view of the inside.

Bake for 35–40 minutes until the pastry is cooked. Sprinkle the garnish ingredients over the top, then serve.

Takes 45 minutes
Serves 4

ASPARAGUS | *Plant crowns any time from late autumn, but be prepared for the long haul. Asparagus will crop for up to 20 years but is relatively unproductive in its first season. Best planted with a sprinkle of sea salt (as it evolved from a marine vegetable).*

Sorrel Pesto

Sorrel is very lemony and makes a fantastic change from basil pesto. It is amazing with anything that suits lemon, like lamb, seafood or chicken, or as part of an antipasto platter.

4 cups sorrel leaves
¼ cup pinenuts
50g parmesan, grated
¼ cup cold-pressed olive oil
½ teaspoon salt
1 teaspoon cracked black pepper
2 teaspoons red wine vinegar

Place all ingredients in a blender and pulse until a granular paste is formed.

Takes 5 minutes
Makes 1 cup

SORREL | *Plant seedlings in a moist bed and harvest the fresh young leaves. Sorrel will bolt to seed in the summer and, if left, will self-seed happily. A carefree and happy producer as long as it is well watered.*

Sorrel Pesto

Green Garlic & Almond Pork Terrine

Remarkably elegant when sliced, this terrine is exceptionally good for picnics, gifts, platters, starters and weekends away.

50g butter
1 onion, finely chopped
1 cup milk
1 bay leaf
1 sprig of rosemary
1 head of green garlic, sliced
(or 4 peeled cloves of garlic, sliced)
½ cup blanched almonds
½ cup fresh white breadcrumbs
700g pork loin, minced (ask the butcher to mince, or pulse in a food processor)
2 extra sprigs of rosemary
1 extra bay leaf
12-16 slices thin-cut streaky bacon

Preheat the oven to 160°C.

Melt the butter in a small saucepan and gently cook the onion to soften before adding the milk, bay leaf, rosemary, green garlic and almonds. Bring the milk nearly to boiling point and then set aside to infuse for 10 minutes.

Remove the bay leaves from the milk and combine the milk with the breadcrumbs and pork mince.

Lay each piece of bacon on a chopping board and run the back of a knife along it to stretch.

Place the 2 sprigs of rosemary and the bay leaf in the loaf or terrine pan and then line with the bacon, allowing enough overhang to cover the pork mixture. Spoon in the pork mixture and fold the bacon over. Wrap the entire pan in recycled foil or wrap tightly in baking paper.

Place the prepared terrine in a high-sided roasting dish and gently pour enough cold water into the roasting dish to come halfway up the terrine pan. Cook in the oven for 2 hours.

Remove the foil or paper and allow the terrine to cool before chilling and cutting.

Takes 2½ hours, plus chilling time
Serves 8

GREEN GARLIC | *Garlic is traditionally planted on the shortest day and harvested on the longest day of the year. Pulling a few bulbs early is a true gardener's treat, as green garlic is still only rarely sold. The flower heads are also delicious sprinkled through salads.*

Green Garlic & Almond Pork Terrine

Cardamom & Mint Stuffed Spring Vine Leaves

Stuffed vine leaves or dolmades are great to make in advance, as they are generally served chilled. They are a lovely thing to do when the spring has reinvigorated grapevines.

½ cup jasmine rice
50g butter
4 cardamom pods
1 teaspoon lemon zest
½ teaspoon mineral salt and freshly ground black pepper to taste
1 small onion, finely chopped
1 tablespoon mint, chopped
1 tablespoon parsley, chopped
12 large grape leaves
2 cups chicken or vegetable stock
1 bay leaf
4 tablespoons natural yoghurt
more chopped herbs to serve

Cook the rice in ample salted water for 10 minutes until tender. Drain well.

Melt the butter in a saucepan and gently cook the cardamom, lemon zest, salt, pepper and onion, then mix through the cooked rice with the chopped herbs.

Bring a large pot of salted water to the boil and use tongs to plunge the grape leaves into the boiling water for about 20 seconds to soften. Lay each leaf flat on a clean board.

Place a spoonful of the rice mixture in the centre of each leaf, tuck the tip, base and sides of the leaf over the rice and roll into tight little sealed parcels. Give each one a little squeeze and fasten with kitchen string. Place fold-side down in a deep-sided frying pan or a medium-sized saucepan.

Pour over the stock and add the bay leaf. Cover the pan with a small plate; this will weigh down the vine leaf parcels in the stock. Simmer for around 20 minutes before draining and chilling.

Serve with a slick of yoghurt and fresh herbs.

Takes 1 hour, plus chilling time
Serves 4

Orange-scented Prawn Tortellini

Orange-scented Prawn Tortellini

A light first course or spring lunch, these delicate morsels bring summer singing to the kitchen table.

200g large raw prawns, peeled, heads and tails removed
1 pinch chilli flakes
3 tablespoons cream or a little egg white
3 small spring onions, green part only
½ teaspoon mineral salt
½ a navel orange, zest only
400g fresh egg pasta (page 154), rolled as for lasagne but not left to dry
1 egg white, extra
olive oil, spring onion and chopped tomato to garnish

Combine the prawns, chilli flakes, cream, spring onions, salt and orange zest in a food processor and pulse to create a chunky mousse. Alternatively, chop all ingredients finely and combine with a little cream or egg white.

Sprinkle flour on a clean benchtop and lay out the pasta. Cut into 5cm squares. Place a spoonful of mixture in the centre of each square, brush the outside edges with egg white and fold over into a triangle.

Pinch together the 2 corners of the longer side of the triangle. Allow the finished tortellini to relax for 20 minutes before cooking. (Can be made a day in advance or frozen on a tray then cooked at any time from frozen: double the cooking time.)

Bring a large pot of salted water to the boil and drop in the tortellini. Cook for 3–5 minutes before serving drizzled with olive oil and scattered with spring onion and a little chopped tomato.

Takes 30 minutes
Serves 4

NAVEL ORANGES | *Navel oranges deliver fruit from late winter and into spring. Suitable for home gardens as mature trees can be kept pruned to around 2 metres.*

Chicken, Preserved Lemon & Green Olive Tagine

A tagine is a North African cooking dish with a conical lid; the lid creates a unique convectional heat, producing lovely succulent dishes. Of course if you do not have a tagine, a casserole dish with a lid will suffice. I used to improvise by making a tepee with foil over chopsticks before I got mine.

8-10 boned chicken thighs, skin removed
8 large green olives
1 onion, finely chopped
1 preserved lemon (page 42), rind only, sliced
1 bunch of thyme
2 tablespoons olive oil
1 tablespoon thick dark honey
½ teaspoon salt
½ cup breadcrumbs

Combine the chicken thighs with the olives, onion, preserved lemon rind, thyme, olive oil and honey. Cover and marinate for a minimum of 1 hour.

Remove the upper racks from the oven to make room for the tall conical lid, and preheat to 180°C.

Place the chicken and the marinade in the base of the tagine dish, and sprinkle with the salt and breadcrumbs. Cover with the conical lid and bake for 1 hour.

Spoon the juices over before serving.

Takes 2 hours
Serves 4

Broad Bean & Prawn Pasta with Sorrel

When buying fresh prawns look for intact shells and feelers.

350-400g spaghetti (dried)
¼ cup cold-pressed olive oil
12-15 young broad bean pods, podded and shelled (1 cup of beans)
12 large raw prawns (king prawns are best)
1 lemon, juice and zest
mineral salt and black pepper
6 large sorrel leaves, sliced (or dill and flat-leaf parsley)
lemon wedges to serve

Cook the spaghetti in ample boiling salted water for 10 minutes until just tender. Drain.

Heat the oil in a large frying pan, add the broad beans and cook for 1 minute before adding the prawns, lemon juice and zest, salt and pepper. Cook for 2–3 minutes until opaque.

Add the sorrel leaves and the cooked pasta, toss together and serve with lemon wedges.

Takes 10 minutes
Serves 4

BROAD BEANS | *Broad beans are spring – the first exciting crop of the year's bounty. Plant in winter and pinch out the growing tips when they start flowering, to discourage whitefly and make the plant bush out. Harvest the pods when about a hand's length. Save seeds for future crops or to use in winter soups and stews.*

Chicken, Preserved Lemon & Green Olive Tagine.
Overleaf: Broad Bean & Prawn Pasta with Sorrel

Anchovy & Rosemary Roasted Leg of Spring Lamb

A good butcher will supply spring lamb, and a superb one will supply milk lamb, preferably with one week's aging. The timing of spring lamb will vary annually so keep in touch with your butcher if you are after a real treat.

2kg leg of spring lamb, shank end removed and trimmed
4 anchovy fillets and 1 tablespoon of the anchovy oil, reserved
2 cloves garlic, cut into slivers
1 large stalk of rosemary
¼ cup fresh breadcrumbs
black pepper

Preheat the oven to 200°C.

Use a small sharp knife to poke holes in the lamb and stuff each of the holes with a portion of the anchovies, garlic slivers and rosemary leaves.

Brush over the reserved anchovy oil and sprinkle with breadcrumbs and black pepper.

Place the lamb in a roasting dish and cook uncovered for 1½ hours.

Remove from the oven and rest, covered with foil and a clean teatowel, for 25 minutes before carving.

Takes 1 hour 40 minutes
Serves 4-6

Note: The general rule for roasting is 30 minutes per 500g plus 20 minutes extra. This recipe specifies 25 minutes per 500g plus the resting time, which allows for an evenly cooked, medium-rare roast that is suited to delicate spring lamb.

Line-caught Fish Roasted in Chive, Parsley & Pink Peppercorn Butter

This herb butter also works well on any white meat - smear it on free-range pork chops before grilling, or rub under the skin of a roasting bird.

800-900g firm-fleshed white fish
1 bunch curly parsley
1 bunch of chives
50g softened butter
2 tablespoons canola oil
2 teaspoons sea salt flakes
2 teaspoons pink peppercorns, crushed

Preheat the oven to 220°C.

Wash and dry the fish and cut into 4 finger-length pieces.

Finely chop the parsley and chives and combine with the butter, oil, salt and pink peppercorns.

Lightly oil a baking rack and place inside a roasting dish. Arrange the fish pieces on the rack and smear with two thirds of the butter mixture. Keep the remaining butter to serve.

Roast for 5–7 minutes depending on the thickness of the fish.

Remove from the oven and cover with foil and a teatowel to allow the fish to finish cooking in its own residual heat for another 5 minutes.

Serve with Chorizo, Caraway & Green Pea Pod Paella (page 94).

Takes 15 minutes
Serves 4

CHIVES | *Growing chives at home is simple – they thrive in spring and survive all year round. They have pretty balls of purple flowers that attract bees and are delicious crumbled in salads. Chives are also handy as a companion plant dotted around the garden, as their oniony smell helps to deter pests.*

Line-caught Fish Roasted in Chive, Parsley & Pink Peppercorn Butter

Parmesan & Tarragon Crusted Chicken Schnitzel

French tarragon has a strong flavour that becomes stronger when it is dried.

2 chicken breasts, halved horizontally
¾ cup flour
1 teaspoon mineral salt and
1 teaspoon white pepper
2 eggs, beaten
¼ cup water
1 cup fresh parmesan, finely grated
1 cup dried breadcrumbs
2 tablespoons French tarragon leaves, chopped (or 2 teaspoons dried tarragon)
8 tablespoons canola oil
1 tablespoon of capers and
4 lemon wedges to serve

Preheat the oven to 200°C.

Place the chicken pieces on a clean board, cover with waxed paper and bash with a rolling pin to flatten so that they are even, like a thick schnitzel.

Prepare three large dishes with the following ingredients: one with combined flour, salt and pepper; one with the beaten eggs and water; and one with the combined parmesan, breadcrumbs and tarragon.

Coat the chicken pieces first in the flour, then the egg, then the crumb mixture. Repeat, so that each piece has been coated twice.

Heat 2 tablespoons of the oil in a large frying pan and fry the first piece of chicken until golden on each side. Place on a baking tray while cooking the remaining pieces.

When all the chicken pieces are fried until golden, place in the oven for 10–15 minutes until cooked through.

Serve with Handmade Herb Mayonnaise (page 78), and fresh rocket.

Takes 30 minutes
Serves 4

FRENCH TARRAGON | *French tarragon is far superior in flavour to Russian tarragon and is the one to plant. The French variety is also easier to grow as it forms more of a bush, whereas the Russian variety can be a bit straggly. Tarragon is deciduous – don't pull it out when it loses its leaves, as they will regrow in the spring.*

Parmesan & Tarragon Crusted Chicken Schnitzel

Seared Rare Beef Cold Plate

This cold plate is perfect when spring finally warms up and a few new potatoes have been smuggled out from beneath the plants. A pre-prepared cold plate is a gardener's delight after a full day's planting and weeding.

500g eye fillet of beef
1 tablespoon peanut oil
12 small new potatoes, boiled and chilled
¼ cup herb mayonnaise (page 78)
1 handful small rocket leaves and edible flowers (eg nasturtium, chive flowers, calendula or borage)

Trim the eye fillet.

Heat a large frying pan and add the oil. Fry the meat for 1 minute on each side, rolling it in the pan to create an even brown crust. Remove from the pan and chill.

Mix the new potatoes with the herb mayonnaise until well coated.

To serve, slice the steak finely and place on a platter with the potatoes and fresh spring leaves and flowers.

Takes 7 minutes, plus chilling time
Serves 4

Gnocchi with Early Basil & Bacon

Gnocchi is possibly the best thing to do with a glut of potatoes. It is not only delicious, it is versatile and can be served as a side or a meal in itself.

1kg floury potatoes
2 egg yolks
50g parmesan, grated
1 cup stoneground flour, sifted
100g bacon, chopped and cooked till crisp
1 cup baby basil leaves
20g parmesan, finely grated

Peel the potatoes and cut into quarters. Boil in salted water for 30 minutes. Strain into a colander and allow to steam off until nice and dry, then push through a sieve or a ricer into a large mixing bowl.

Beat the yolks and parmesan into the potatoes with a wooden spoon and then stir in the flour, a tablespoon or two at a time, until a firm dough is formed.

Knead the dough on the bench top with the remaining flour. Divide the dough into 4 and roll each section into a fat worm about 2cm thick. Cut into 2–3cm lengths and mark each gnocchi with a flour-dipped fork. Squeeze each one gently into a little hump.

Spread the gnocchi out on a floured oven tray and rest for at least 10 minutes or until ready to cook.

To cook, bring a large pot of salted water to the boil. Drop the gnocchi into the water in batches and bring back to the boil. Remove the gnocchi when they have risen to the surface.

Serve with the bacon, basil leaves and parmesan.

Takes 1 hour
Serves 4-6

Note: Gnocchi freeze well and can be cooked from frozen; they may take a little longer, but as with fresh gnocchi, are ready when they rise to the surface.

Gnocchi with Early Basil & Bacon

Rhubarb & Coconut Mess

Smashed meringues with fruit and cream form the basis of the delightful dessert, called 'Eton Mess' as it is said to be a favourite at the illustrious British boys school of the same name.

6-8 stalks rhubarb
1 tablespoon caster sugar
2 tablespoons water
2 egg whites
1 pinch cream of tartar, or a drop or two of lemon juice
110g caster sugar, extra
¼ cup toasted coconut threads
200ml cream, whipped

Preheat the oven to 150°C.

Roughly chop the rhubarb and mix with the tablespoon of caster sugar and the water. Place in an ovenproof dish with a lid and bake for 20 minutes until the rhubarb is soft to the touch. Chill, retaining any juices until ready to assemble.

Lower the oven temperature to 110°C. Line a baking tray with baking paper.

Whisk the egg whites with the cream of tartar or lemon juice until stiff. Keep whisking and slowly incorporate half of the sugar until shiny. Fold through the remaining sugar.

Drop spoonfuls of the mixture onto the prepared tray. Bake for 2 hours, until the meringues are dried out and lift easily from the paper. Transfer to a wire rack and leave to cool completely.

Break the meringues into pieces. To serve, combine the rhubarb, coconut, cream and the meringue pieces. Pile into glasses or bowls.

Takes 3 hours 15 minutes, or 15 minutes with pre-made meringues
Serves 4

Rose Fool

A fool is really just flavour suspended in a creamy substance – this could be a purée suspended in a custard or cream. This delicate rose fool benefits from the sharpness of a little yoghurt.

½ cup water
1 tablespoon rosewater
½ cup sugar
1-2 drops natural red food colouring (optional)
1 cup yoghurt
1 cup cream
rose petals (spray-free)
icing sugar

Combine the water, rosewater, sugar and food colouring in a small saucepan and dissolve over a low heat without stirring. This should take at least 10 minutes. Cool.

Combine the cooled rose syrup with the yoghurt.

Beat the cream till firm and fold through the yoghurt mixture. Spoon into serving dishes and chill. Top with rose petals and sprinkle with icing sugar before serving.

Takes 15 minutes, plus cooling time
Serves 4

ROSES | *Our neighbour's rambling rose hangs over our fence. It is one of the finest displays of spring, and a mecca for honeybees. Any plant that attracts honeybees is valuable to a garden as the bee is essential for much propagation.*

Rose Fool

Last Year's Jam & White Chocolate Sponge Roll

Before the summer fruit is ripe and jam-making starts in earnest, any jam left from the previous summer can be used up in this yummy sponge roll.

200g white chocolate
1 teaspoon vanilla extract
5 eggs, separated
100g caster sugar
1 tablespoon flour
¼ teaspoon baking powder
50g caster sugar, extra
¾ cup any jam
200ml cream

Preheat the oven to 200°C.

Melt the chocolate with the vanilla extract in a small bowl set over a saucepan of boiling water.

Beat the egg yolks with 50g of the caster sugar until light and fluffy and then fold in the melted chocolate. Sift the flour and baking powder over and stir through.

Beat the egg whites until firm but not dry, slowly adding the remaining 50g of caster sugar. Add a large spoonful of beaten egg white to the egg yolk and chocolate mixture and stir to loosen before folding through the remaining egg whites.

Pour into a roasting pan that has been lined with a double layer of baking paper. Bake for 15–20 minutes until just set.

Slide the cake onto a wire rack and cover with a clean damp cloth to stop it from cracking as it cools.

Lay a clean teatowel on the benchtop, scatter it with caster sugar and flip the cake top-side down onto the cloth. Spread the cake with jam and then whipped cream and roll up tightly, using the teatowel to keep it firm.

Takes 40 minutes, plus cooling time
Serves 8

Carrot, Cardamom & Pinenut Cake

This dense tea cake is very moist and will easily keep for a week in an airtight container.

¾ cup sunflower oil
4 eggs, beaten
1 cup soft dark brown sugar, firmly packed
1½ cups spring carrots, grated
1 cup roughly chopped walnuts, pinenuts and raisins
1½ cups plain flour
1½ teaspoons baking powder
½ teaspoon baking soda
1½ teaspoons ground cardamom
1 teaspoon cinnamon
¼ teaspoon ginger

Preheat the oven to 170°C and line a 20cm deep springform cake pan with baking paper.

Beat together the oil, eggs and sugar.

Fold through the grated carrots, nuts and raisins and sifted flour, baking powder and baking soda. Then add the cardamom, cinnamon and ginger.

Pour into the prepared pan and bake for 40 minutes.

Run a knife around the outside edge of the cake to release it from the pan before opening the springform clip. Leave to cool before icing.

Takes 50 minutes
Serves 8-10

Note: I hardly ever ice this cake – I simply dust it with demerara sugar and cinnamon while still warm and serve with yoghurt.

White Chocolate & Bay Mousse

Bay leaf is an essential part of a bouquet garni in a soup or stew - but it is also great to use in desserts made with milk, as its lively sweetness gives an interesting flavour.

100ml milk
3 bay leaves, broken in half
200g white chocolate, broken into chunks
200ml cream
2 egg whites
cracked black pepper

Heat the milk with the bay leaves until almost boiling. Remove from the heat and leave to infuse for 10 minutes.

Strain out the bay leaves and add the chocolate to the milk. Heat very gently while stirring until the chocolate is melted. Do not let it boil. Pour into a large bowl and chill.

Beat the cream and fold through the milk and white chocolate mixture.

Beat the egg whites and fold through. Divide the mixture between individual serving dishes and chill for at least 2 hours until firm. Serve with a grind of black pepper.

Takes 20 minutes, plus 2 hours chilling time
Serves 6

BAY TREES | *If you have a bay tree, the leaves can be harvested all year. They will grow in a pot, but need to be repotted as they grow. Plant at the end of spring to make the most of the summer growing season. Bay leaves are said to ward off weevils: I keep a bay leaf or two in my flour, rice and breadcrumb jars and I have never had a problem.*

Bottled Rhubarb

This rhubarb is bottled in a very light sugar syrup to prevent it from becoming too sweet over time in the jar.

1 cup sugar
3 cups water
24 stalks of rhubarb, washed and sliced

Put the sugar in a large saucepan and gently pour in the water. Slowly bring to the boil to dissolve the sugar without stirring. Simmer for 10 minutes. Allow to cool.

Tightly pack the rhubarb into clean wet jars. Pour in the cooled syrup; insert a palate knife down each side to help release the air bubbles. Allow the syrup to overflow before placing the dome seal on top and screwing on the band.

Use a large stockpot that is deep enough so that you can cover the jars with water. Line the pot with a teatowel. Place the jars on the teatowel, slightly apart so that they are not touching. Pour enough water over to cover the jars. Bring the water to the boil and simmer gently for 30 minutes.

Remove the jars and allow to cool before removing the screwbands.

Takes 45 minutes
Makes 2 x 750ml jars

Tangelo Cordial

This cordial is an intense and rich orange. The flavour of the tangelos is like a cross between sweet tangerine and bitter pomelo. Tangelos are very juicy and are best eaten outside, leaning forward, with a teatowel to catch the drips.

10 tangelos
3 cups sugar
1 litre water
2 teaspoons tartaric acid
1 teaspoon citric acid

Use a potato peeler or a zester to remove the zest from 3 of the tangelos before juicing all of them. Remove and discard the bitter white pith from the zest.

Put the juice and zest in a large non-reactive pot (enamel or stainless steel), and add the sugar, water, tartaric and citric acids.

Bring to the boil and keep at a rolling boil for 10 minutes.

Allow to cool before straining and pouring into sterilised bottles.

Takes 25 minutes
Makes 1.5 litres

TANGELOS | *It's not worth rushing the early tangelos; they have a more consistent flavour mid season.*

Bottled Rhubarb
Overleaf (left) Tangelo Cordial;
(right) Handmade Herb Mayonnaise

Handmade Herb Mayonnaise

2 egg yolks, at room temperature
1 teaspoon Dijon mustard
3 cloves garlic, crushed
1 pinch mineral salt and 1 pinch white pepper
300ml canola oil
1 tablespoon boiling water
½ teaspoon red wine vinegar
1 cup dill, basil and flat-leaf parsley leaves, finely chopped

In a medium-sized bowl beat together the egg yolks, mustard, garlic, salt and pepper.

Place the canola oil in a jug and very slowly drip into the yolk mix while whisking furiously. Whisk in the boiling water and a dash of red wine vinegar. Fold through the chopped herbs.

Takes 10 minutes
Makes 1½ cups

Salsa Verde with Orange

This traditional Italian parsley salsa has more warmth when made with orange rather than lemon. Use as you would pesto, on cheeseboards or accompanying white meats.

1 thick slice white bread, crusts removed
⅓ cup cold-pressed olive oil
4 cornichons or very small gherkins, diced
1 anchovy
2 cups parsley, chopped
1 clove garlic, crushed
½ teaspoon black pepper
zest of ½ an orange
juice of 1 orange
a little extra olive oil if required

Soak the white bread in the olive oil until soft and pulpy.

Add the cornichons, anchovy, parsley, garlic, pepper, orange zest and juice. Blend until smooth using a stick blender or in a small food processor.

Blend in a little more olive oil to achieve the right consistency.

Takes 5 minutes
Makes 1¼ cups

Mint & Rosemary Jelly

2kg apples, roughly chopped
1½ cups water
¼ cup fresh mint leaves, chopped
1 tablespoon rosemary leaves, chopped
1 cup malt vinegar
¾ cup sugar
1 teaspoon rosemary leaves

Put the apples, water, mint and first quantity of rosemary into a large saucepan and bring to the boil. Simmer for 30 minutes.

Place a large sieve over a large bowl, line with the larger piece of muslin and strain in the fruit pulp. Tie the muslin into a bundle and suspend over the bowl to catch the liquid. Leave overnight.

Discard the fruit pulp and pour the liquid into a saucepan. Add the vinegar and sugar and bring to the boil, stirring until the sugar dissolves. Boil rapidly until a drop of the liquid on a saucer wrinkles when tilted, or a sugar thermometer reads between 104°C and 107°C.

Stir through the remaining rosemary and pour into sterilised jars. Cover when set.

Takes 1 hour over 2 days
Makes 4 jars

MINT | *Mint grows like a weed in most gardens and can be harvested all year. It is best, however, when there has been plenty of rain, as the moist earth makes for prolific growth.*

Tangelo & Mint Tisane

1 large handful of mint leaves
1 tangelo, juice and zest
1 heaped teaspoon jasmine tea
500ml boiling water
1 heaped teaspoon grated palm sugar (optional)

Scrunch and roughly chop the mint and combine with the tangelo juice and zest. Top with the jasmine tea and pour the boiling water over. Sweeten with palm sugar for a caramel flavour that offsets the mint.

Stir and allow to steep for 3 minutes before serving.

Takes 5 minutes
Makes 2 cups

summer

Summer is hot and sticky, damp and humid; it threatens plants with mould or drought, steals appetites, and pushes out the dinner hour past children's bedtime. In the summer garden, lettuces and herbs race to set seed, placing the sun-soaked gardener on constant watch. Light dressings adorn crisp salad leaves, and jugs of iced cordial are kept ready to quench the gardener's thirst.

a summer menu

LUNCH IN THE GARDEN

- Tomato Salad with Fennel Seed Vinaigrette
- Charred Spring Onions with Grana Padano
- Chorizo, Caraway & Green Pea Pod Paella
- Chicken en Crapaudine with Fines Herbes & Mustard
- Grilled Nectarines with Vanilla Mascarpone & Almonds
- Raspberry Leaf & Chamomile Flower Tea

busy in the summer garden

TIME TO PLANT

- asparagus
- aubergine
- basil
- beans
- broccoli
- beetroot
- cabbage
- cape gooseberries
- capsicum
- carrots
- celeriac
- chilli
- chives
- coriander
- courgettes
- cucumber
- globe artichokes
- leeks
- lettuce
- parsley
- parsnips
- peas
- potatoes
- pumpkin
- radishes
- rockmelon
- shallots
- silverbeet
- spring onions
- sunflower
- sweetcorn
- tomato plants
- watermelon

TIME TO HARVEST

- capsicum
- tomatoes
- Valencia oranges
- herbs
- courgettes
- sweetcorn
- peas
- potatoes
- pumpkin
- radishes
- berries
- stonefruit
- shallots
- silverbeet
- cabbage
- gherkins
- crab apples
- garlic
- onions
- beetroot

TIME TO TEND

- check capsicum stakes
- tend tomato plants, pulling out tips and shoots from the elbows
- remove seedheads from early bolting herbs such as coriander
- net raspberry canes and strawberry plants
- get planting
- keep weeding

Tomato Salad with Fennel Seed Vinaigrette

Nothing can be simpler than a salad of sliced tomatoes fresh from the garden with a slick of well-flavoured dressing.

2 tablespoons red wine vinegar
¼ cup olive oil
1 teaspoon thick raw honey
2 teaspoons toasted fennel seeds
6 large beefsteak or heirloom tomatoes
sea salt

Combine the dressing ingredients and leave overnight for the fennel flavour to permeate the oil.

Slice the tomatoes into large slices, discarding the tops.

Arrange the tomato slices and sprinkle liberally with sea salt.

Beat the dressing quickly with a fork before drizzling over the tomato slices. If time allows, chill for 10 minutes before serving with hunks of grilled olive oil bread (page 155).

Takes 10 minutes, plus chilling time
Serves 4

TOMATOES | *Finally, after they have been sitting on the windowsill and moving into progressively larger pots all spring, it is time to plant them out. Plant the tallest stakes at the same time and tie in as they grow, nipping out any growth in the elbows of the plants and pulling any leaves that are dragging on the ground or crowding out other plants.*

Dill & Preserved Lemon Gravlax

A plate of finely sliced gravlax is an elegant first course. It also makes a luxurious open sandwich on a slice of brown bread.

500g side of salmon, skin removed
4 tablespoons coarse sea salt
2 tablespoons soft brown sugar
1 large bunch dill, chopped
1 preserved lemon (page 42), rind only, sliced
2 tablespoons crème fraîche
1 tablespoon horseradish sauce
baby salad leaves or herbs

Wash and dry the salmon and place on a baking tray. Cover with sea salt, brown sugar, dill and preserved lemon rind. Cover with another baking tray and a heavy weight (I use a couple of my biggest cookbooks).

Leave in the fridge for 2 days before removing, wiping with a clean cloth and slicing finely.

Combine the crème fraîche and horseradish and add a little salt to taste. Serve the salmon with the horseradish and baby salad or herb leaves.

Takes 2 days
Serves 4

Note: Kept well wrapped in plastic wrap in the fridge, gravlax will keep for up to 2 weeks.

DILL | *Dill is in full flush in early summer but will quickly bolt to seed; luckily the flower heads and seeds are equally delicious.*

Dill & Preserved Lemon Gravlax

Pear, Pecorino & Walnut Salsa

½ cup walnut halves

1 pear

75g pecorino cheese

1 teaspoon fresh thyme leaves

2 tablespoons cold-pressed extra virgin olive oil

Preheat the oven to 200°C and toast the walnuts for 5–7 minutes. When cool enough to handle, rub between your fingers or in a clean teatowel to remove most of the loose skin. Break each half into large chunks.

Peel and dice the pear. Toss with the walnuts, crumbled pecorino and thyme in the olive oil.

Serve over a simply cooked chicken breast, or as part of a platter.

Takes 10 minutes
Makes 1½ cups

PEARS | *Pears will tolerate a wide range of soils and will grow in wetter conditions than apple trees, but they are not fond of frosts. It is best to plant a second pear tree nearby to ensure good fruit.*

Grilled Courgette & Cherry Tomato Salad

There is nothing difficult about this salad. It is best with cherry tomatoes freshly picked and still warm from the sun. It makes a great topping for grilled French bread with a slick of homemade herb mayonnaise (page 78) as a bright and tasty lunch.

8 small courgettes, halved lengthwise

4 small yellow or red capsicums, seeds removed and quartered

2 tablespoons cold-pressed olive oil

½ teaspoon salt

12 cherry tomatoes, halved

10 basil leaves

1 tablespoon balsamic vinegar (the thick and sweet kind)

Toss the courgettes and capsicums in the olive oil and salt. Grill on a griddle pan or barbecue plate until just softened and nicely browned.

Toss together with the cherry tomatoes and basil leaves and drizzle with balsamic vinegar.

Takes 15 minutes
Serves 4

COURGETTES | *Plant courgette seedlings in full sun on little mounds of earth to support the stems. Pick regularly to keep them producing and to prevent all the plant's energy from going into growing one large marrow. Small courgettes picked fresh from the garden are firm and filled with flavour, and fantastic simply grilled as part of a warm salad in summer months.*

Pear, Pecorino & Walnut Salsa

Pea & Parsley Soup with Scallops

The bright green of this soup certainly gives it a wow factor! If scallops are not available try serving it with fried bacon cubes – or toasted macadamia nuts as a vegetarian option.

50g butter
1 large onion, finely sliced
2 stalks celery, finely chopped
1 bay leaf
3 cups vegetable or chicken stock
2 teaspoons mineral salt, finely ground
1kg peas, freshly picked and shelled
 (or use frozen peas)
1 cup finely chopped parsley
¾ cup cream
½ teaspoon white pepper
2 teaspoons red wine vinegar
50g butter
1 pinch mineral salt, finely ground
18 scallops
5 leaves tarragon

Melt the butter in a large saucepan, add the onion and celery with the bay leaf and slowly cook for about 10 minutes.

Add the stock and the salt (if using bought stock, taste before adding salt). Bring to the boil, then add the peas and cover to bring back to the boil quickly.

Boil for 3 minutes until the peas are vibrant green. Remove from the heat and stir through the parsley, cream and white pepper. Blend using a stick blender. Taste and add the red wine vinegar and more salt if required. Keep warm while cooking the scallops.

Heat the butter in a heavy frying pan, sprinkle with a little mineral salt. Fry the scallops with the tarragon for 1–2 minutes on each side.

To serve, pour the soup into bowls and place the scallops. Top with the fried tarragon and drizzle with the pan juices.

Takes 20 minutes
Serves 6

PEAS | *Keep planting peas from spring all through summer to ensure a good supply. Pick regularly as this encourages the plants to keep producing.*

Pea & Parsley Soup with Scallops

Spaghetti Marinara with Baby Mustard & Nasturtium Leaves

Mustard and nasturtium are both peppery and hot. They work beautifully with any seafood or subtly flavoured dish, as well as being an unbeatable addition to the humble egg sandwich.

16 fresh cockles
8 small mussels
2 tablespoons white wine vinegar
2 tablespoons olive oil
1 tablespoon sea salt
8 fresh whole tomatoes or ⅔ cup homemade passata (page 110)
1 red onion, cut into 6 wedges
100g firm fish, cut into large chunks
400g spaghetti
½ cup baby mustard leaves, fresh
½ cup sliced nasturtium leaves, fresh
nasturtium flowers to decorate

Scrub the cockles, put in a bowl of cold fresh water (not sea water) and leave in the fridge to spit out the sand, for at least a few hours or overnight if you have time.

Scrub the mussels and remove the beards.

Preheat the oven to 250°C.

In an ovenproof casserole dish, combine the vinegar, olive oil, salt, tomatoes, onion wedges, cockles and mussels. Cover with a lid and roast for 10 minutes. Add the fish and cook for another 5 minutes with the lid on.

Cook the spaghetti while the seafood is roasting.

Press the tomatoes with a wooden spoon to release the juices. Add the mustard and nasturtium leaves and the drained cooked spaghetti to the casserole and roughly stir before serving.

Takes 25 minutes
Serves 4

MUSTARD LEAVES | *Plant mustard in spring and harvest for this dish while still young. It is a fast germinator so can be grown on and replenished quickly. Dig what you don't use back in to return the nitrogen to the soil.*

Charred Spring Onions with Grana Padano

This recipe may seem unusual, but grilling spring onions brings out their natural sweetness.

¼ cup olive oil
2 tablespoons vino cotto (cooked grape must syrup)
1 teaspoon salt
25 spring onions, roots and most of the green shoot removed
50g grana padano cheese, finely grated
1 tablespoon capers, rinsed

Combine the olive oil, vino cotto and salt as a dressing, and toss the spring onions in the dressing.

Leave to marinate for at least 1 hour or overnight.

Heat a chargrill pan or barbecue until smoking hot.

Chargrill the spring onions until limp and partly blackened. Take care to turn them regularly.

Serve with the grated cheese and capers.

Takes 1 hour 20 minutes
Serves 4-6

SPRING ONIONS | *Spring onions are not aptly named, as in reality they never seem to be of the store-bought size until the summer. Plant on the shortest day along with other alliums (onion/garlic family) and be prepared to cover with cloches while young (old jam jars work well for this). They may be a long wait, but planted between rows of carrots they confuse many of the root crop pests so it is good to have them grown on before carrot planting time (leave lots of room though, as carrot tops do cast a bit of a shadow).*

*Charred Spring Onions with Grana Padano
Overleaf: (right) Chorizo, Caraway &
Green Pea Pod Paella*

Chorizo, Caraway
& Green Pea Pod Paella

20 pods freshly picked peas, or ¾ cup peas
(defrosted if frozen)
2 tablespoons cold-pressed olive oil
1 onion, finely chopped
3 cloves garlic, crushed
2 teaspoons mineral salt
2 teaspoons caraway seeds, toasted
100g chorizo, sliced
1 cup calasparra rice
2 cups organic chicken or vegetable stock
1 tablespoon red wine vinegar

Shell some of the peas, but leave some of the
smallest pods whole as they are edible too.

Heat the oil in a paella pan with a 23cm diameter
base. Gently cook the onion for 5 minutes before
adding the garlic, salt, caraway seeds and chorizo.
Increase the heat and cook until fragrant. Add
the rice and toast for 2 minutes.

Reduce the heat to low and pour in the stock
and vinegar. Cover and leave to cook gently. After
10 minutes give the pan a gentle shake, taking
care not to slop anything over the sides. Avoid
stirring, as this will prevent a crust forming on
the bottom.

After another 10 minutes add the peas and pea
pods (or thawed peas), cover again and remove
from the heat. Rest for 5 minutes, letting the heat
of the rice cook the peas before serving.

Takes 35 minutes
Serves 4

GREEN PEAS | *When planting peas, there
are two basic varieties: the smooth-skinned and
the wrinkly skinned. Plant the smooth-skinned
ones in succession all the way through spring
to ensure a good supply of peas to pick in the
summer months. The wrinkly-looking pea seed is
more suited to late spring and summer planting.
After they have finished producing, cut the vines
off at ground level and leave the roots in the
ground to replenish the soil with nitrogen.*

Whole Grilled Fish
with Coriander

1–1.2kg line-caught fish, scaled and gutted
1 teaspoon sea salt
4cm knob ginger, sliced
2 bunches coriander including roots, chopped
3 spring onions, chopped
¼ cup light soy sauce
2 tablespoons honey
2 teaspoons sesame oil

Slit the fish open along the gut, remove the gills,
wash and dry thoroughly.

Sprinkle the inside of the cavity with sea salt.

Stuff with the ginger, coriander and spring onions.
Seal the belly again by threading through a large
metal skewer. Make three deep slits in the fish on
both sides.

Brush with the combined soy sauce, honey and
sesame oil. Barbecue or grill for 5–7 minutes on
each side, continuing to brush regularly with the
soy mixture.

Place on a large warm platter and drizzle with
the remaining soy baste. Cover with foil and rest
for 5 minutes before serving.

Takes 20 minutes
Serves 4

CORIANDER | *Coriander by this time of
year is bolting to flower and seed. Plant some
in partial shade to slow this process and water
a little every day – but really it is just a race
against nature. Once the seeds have formed,
harvest the long stems and hang upside down in
a paper bag to catch the falling coriander seeds
for the spice cupboard and continual sowing.*

Whole Grilled Fish with Coriander

Chicken en Crapaudine with Fines Herbes & Mustard

The chicken is spatchcocked (cut down the backbone and splayed), so it does look a little toadish (crapaud means 'toad' in French).

50g butter, softened
¼ cup olive oil
¼ cup parsley leaves (flat-leaf or curly), chopped
1 bunch chives, chopped
1 tablespoon tarragon leaves, chopped
¼ cup chervil leaves, chopped
1 size 14 chicken
2 teaspoons sea salt and 1 teaspoon crushed black pepper
1 tablespoon flat-leaf parsley leaves, chopped
½ cup dried breadcrumbs

Mix together the butter, olive oil, parsley, chives, tarragon and chervil.

Wash and dry the bird and then tuck the wing tips back under the wing. Place the bird breast side down on the chopping board, with the parson's nose (the tail end) facing you. Use a pair of sharp scissors or a sharp knife blade (not the tip) to cut along one side of the backbone.

Spread the chicken out and place your hand under the skin from the neck end to loosen (a little like putting on a glove). Spread the herb butter mixture onto the chicken flesh beneath the skin.

Salt and pepper the skin of the chicken liberally and sprinkle over the parsley and breadcrumbs, pressing them to help them stick.

Place the chicken breast side up on a preheated barbecue rack and cook with the lid closed for 45 minutes. (If cooking in the oven, preheat to 220°C and cook for 45–50 minutes.) Rest for 15 minutes under foil.

Cut into rough sections to serve.

Takes 75 minutes
Serves 4

FINES HERBES | *These traditional soft summer herbs have similar growing habits. They like moist premium soil that is loamy with great drainage and plenty of sun. Use on a cut and come again basis, and cut out any flowering heads to prevent them bolting to seed.*

Chicken en Crapaudine with Fines Herbes & Mustard
Overleaf: (left) Blackened Spice Lamb Fillets

Blackened Spice Lamb Fillets

This basic spice combination comes from a goat curry that was on the menu in a tapas restaurant where I worked. It works beautifully with lamb. The warmth of the spices combined with the cool crisp dressing is like a sea breeze on a summer evening.

2 tablespoons ground cinnamon
1 tablespoon ground cumin
1 tablespoon ground coriander
2 teaspoons black pepper, finely ground
1 tablespoon mineral salt, finely ground
4 lamb backstraps (loin)
1 cucumber, peeled and sliced
1 cup mint leaves, chopped
¼ cup thick Greek yoghurt
¼ teaspoon sea salt
2 tablespoons canola oil
1 pinch salt

Combine the spices well and roll the backstraps in the spices.

Cover and chill for 1–4 hours to allow the spices to permeate the meat.

Combine the cucumber, mint, yoghurt and sea salt.

Heat a grill, barbecue or frying pan. Brush the pan with oil and sprinkle with salt before cooking the lamb for 4 minutes on each side. Rest the lamb for 5 minutes under baking paper in a warm place. Cut each backstrap into 3 sections and serve with the cucumber and yoghurt.

Takes 1 hour 13 minutes
Serves 4

Sticky Green Garlic 24-Hour Pork Spare Ribs

The pork spare rib comes from the belly. It is a very inexpensive cut, and fun to eat. The more flavour that can be infused through marinating, the better.

1.5kg pork spare ribs
¼ cup honey
¼ cup light soy sauce
1 bulb green garlic, sliced
2cm green ginger, crushed
1 tablespoon red wine vinegar
2 teaspoons roughly crushed Szechuan pepper (or crushed black pepper)

Place the spare ribs in a roasting dish that will fit in the fridge.

Combine the rest of the ingredients and pour over the spare ribs. Marinate in the fridge for 24 hours, turning when you think of it to keep them evenly coated.

Preheat the oven to 180°C and roast the ribs under foil for 2 hours.

Turn the ribs in their sauce and discard the foil. Increase the oven temperature to 210°C and cook for a further 15 minutes before serving.

Takes 2¼ hours, plus marinating time
Serves 4

GARLIC | *Garlic is a sleeper crop that stores well by simply removing the outer papery layer, tying the long leaves together and allowing to dry. Fresh garlic pulled before the longest day can be washed and used as green garlic: it has a milder, nuttier flavour and the whole bulb is used rather than the individual cloves.*

Roast Sirloin with Rahu Road Salted Cabbage

This salted cabbage recipe comes from a friend who lives up the Rahu in the Waikato region of New Zealand's North Island. It is best made in advance. The beetroot adds a lovely earthy flavour and rich colour, making it a stunning partner for red meat.

¼ cup olive oil

¼ cup wholegrain mustard

2 teaspoons salt and 1 tablespoon coarsely ground black pepper

1-1.5kg whole sirloin, trimmed

2 cloves garlic, sliced lengthwise

1 small white cabbage

2 tablespoons mineral salt

1 large beetroot, grated

2 carrots, grated

2 tablespoons rich, nutty oil (such as macadamia, walnut or flaxseed oil)

Combine the olive oil, mustard, salt and pepper and rub all over the sirloin. Make a few slits in the sirloin with a sharp knife and poke a slice of garlic into each incision.

Cover and rest in the fridge for at least 1 hour. Remove from the fridge a good 20 minutes before cooking to allow it to come to room temperature.

Preheat the oven to 220°C.

Place the sirloin in a roasting pan with a little oil and roast for 35 minutes. Remove from the oven, cover with foil and rest for 15 minutes in a warm place before slicing.

Finely slice the cabbage, place in a colander and sprinkle with the salt. Use tongs to toss and turn the cabbage until it wilts.

Place the cabbage in a serving dish and mix through the beetroot, carrot and nut oil. Chill for at least 20 minutes to allow the colours and flavours to combine. Serve alongside the sliced sirloin.

Takes 2 hours 10 minutes
Serves 4-6

CABBAGE | *The paler cabbages are happier during the hot summer months. Plant larger seedlings out in late winter and keep them well protected from the wind; they'll love the spring rain and will be strong and ready to head up quickly in the summer sun.*

Boiled & Glazed Happy Honey Ham

It is possibly one of the most useful things to have hanging about in the summer: a good glazed ham will fill late-night bread rolls, picnic sandwiches, run off in the sticky fingers of hungry kids or fry up with eggs for a lazy Sunday breakfast. The stock makes a delicious risotto or pea and ham soup.

4.5kg leg joint of ham
2 bay leaves
1 bunch thyme
1 bunch parsley, stalks only
8 black peppercorns
2 carrots, roughly chopped
2 onions, roughly chopped
¼ cup thick dark honey
2 teaspoons soy sauce
1 tablespoon powdered mustard
½ teaspoon ground cloves

Place the ham in a large pot with the bay leaves, thyme, parsley, peppercorns, carrots and onions. Cover with water and bring to the boil. Reduce the heat and simmer for 2¼ to 2½ hours. Remove from the stock and leave until cool enough to handle.

Strain the stock and keep for making soup or risotto.

Make a cut around the thin end of the joint and ease off the skin, leaving a good layer of fat. Score the fat.

Preheat the oven to 220°C.

Combine the honey, soy sauce, mustard and cloves in a small saucepan and heat gently, stirring to combine. When melted and warm, brush all over the scored ham fat until the mixture is all used up.

Bake the ham for 25 minutes or until glossy and caramel in colour.

Takes 3 hours, plus cooling time
Serves 12–15

Note: The cooking time is based on simmering for 25 minutes per 450g; if the joint is much bigger it will need a little less time (20 minutes per 450g), as the residual heat will take longer to cool and will therefore finish the cooking.

Boiled & Glazed Happy Honey Ham

Blueberry Vanilla Tennis Cake

This cake is super large, made in a roasting pan. It is great for cutting into squares to serve to a crowd.

250g butter, softened
2 cups sugar
6 eggs, beaten
4 cups plain flour
4 teaspoons baking powder
½ teaspoon salt
2 cups sour cream or thick Greek yoghurt
2 teaspoons vanilla essence
2 cups blueberries (or 2 punnets)
icing sugar to serve

Preheat the oven to 180°C and grease and line a 335 x 230 x 45mm roasting pan.

In a super-large bowl, cream the butter and sugar together until light and fluffy. Beat in the eggs one at a time.

Sift together the flour, baking powder and salt and add to the mixture alternately with the combined sour cream and vanilla essence. Fold the blueberries through the mixture.

Pour the batter into the prepared pan.

Bake for 45–50 minutes, until a skewer comes out clean when inserted.

When cool, cut into squares and serve dusted with icing sugar.

Takes 1 hour
Serves 16

BLUEBERRIES | *Blueberries like an acidic soil, so I add pine needles as mulch. This does lead to sudden pulling over and leaping out of the car when I see pine trees, but a happy adventure is always had. If you are a pine cone collector or into natural Christmas trees, those are good times to collect pine needles, too. It is important to have more than one blueberry bush if you want a bumper crop.*

Blueberry Vanilla Tennis Cake

Dark Chocolate & Cherry Tart

Dutch Cocoa Pastry

150g stoneground plain flour
2 tablespoons Dutch cocoa
1 pinch salt
100g unsalted butter, softened
3 egg yolks
100g icing sugar
½ teaspoon vanilla extract

Sift the flour, cocoa and salt onto a clean benchtop and make a well in the middle.

Place the softened butter, egg yolks, icing sugar and vanilla extract in the well. Use a palate knife to stir the butter, eggs and sugar together.

Sweep the circle of the palate knife wider to incorporate the flour from around the edges of the well. When the dough has come together, knead briefly and then chill for 20 minutes.

Preheat the oven to 180°C. Roll the pastry out to the required shape, line the tart tin and blind bake (page 153) for 10 minutes. Remove the blind-baking materials and continue to bake the pastry for another 5 minutes.

Chocolate Cherry Filling

½ cup cream
200g dark chocolate, roughly chopped
3 egg yolks
¼ cup caster sugar
200g cherries, stones removed

Preheat the oven to 160°C.

Heat the cream in a small bowl set over a saucepan of boiling water. Add the chocolate and stir until melted.

In a bowl, beat together the egg yolks and caster sugar until pale and fluffy and the caster sugar has dissolved. Fold through the chocolate mixture, along with the cherries.

Pour the filling into the prepared pastry case and bake for 35–40 minutes, until set.

Takes 2 hours
Serves 8-10

Dark Chocolate & Cherry Tart

Grilled Nectarines with Vanilla Mascarpone & Almonds

I like to make these in advance and serve them chilled. If serving hot, a spoonful of ice cream that melts into the fruit is a great alternative to the mascarpone.

2 tablespoons thick dark honey
1 teaspoon balsamic vinegar
1 pinch salt
4 nectarines, halved and stoned
½ cup mascarpone
½ teaspoon vanilla extract
1 tablespoon icing sugar
2 tablespoons sliced almonds, toasted

In a small saucepan melt the honey with the vinegar and pinch of salt.

Place the nectarine halves cut side up in a roasting dish and pour over the honey sauce. Place under a preheated grill or on the barbecue for 7–10 minutes until soft and hot through. Chill for 2 hours.

Combine the mascarpone with the vanilla and icing sugar and place a large spoonful on top of nectarine half.

Serve sprinkled with the toasted almonds.

Takes 10 minutes, plus chilling time
Serves 4

STONEFRUIT | *Most stonefruit needs a frost to set fruit, but low-chill varieties are available. Make sure you buy appropriate plants for your region. Buy bare-rooted specimens in winter, and look for two-year-old trees as they are less expensive and the good root growth will happen in your ground rather than in the container. A second tree nearby will help produce bigger crops.*

Strawberry & Maple Syrup Ice Cream

This requires at least 4 hours' freezing time, so it is best to make it the night before. Meringue-based ice cream is excellent for making fruit purée ice creams, and doesn't require a special ice-cream maker or constant churning and beating.

250g strawberries, washed and chopped
¼ cup maple syrup
300g caster sugar
200ml water
3 egg whites
300ml cream

Mash or purée about one quarter of the strawberries with the maple syrup. Fold through the remaining strawberries.

Place the sugar and water together in a pan and bring to the boil. Boil for 6–7 minutes until it thickens slightly. If you have a sugar thermometer, heat to 120°C.

Use electric beaters to whisk the egg whites in a large bowl. When fluffy, slowly pour in the hot syrup and keep beating until the meringue mixture is firm and thick.

Whisk the cream until thick but still soft, as it is easier to fold together if it's not as thick as the meringue mixture. Fold the 2 mixtures together, then loosely fold in the strawberry mixture.

Pour into a deep baking pan and freeze. Serve when firm.

Takes 20 minutes, plus chilling time
Makes 2 litres

STRAWBERRIES | *Plant a strawberry crop each year, as they perform best in their second year (especially if you can resist letting them fruit in the first year; I hold back two or three plants each year). Transplant the runners from the plants that you have held back, in late summer or early autumn. Surround plants with straw only after the last of the spring rains, to deter slugs and snails.*

Grilled Nectarines with Vanilla Mascarpone & Almonds

Pickled Honey Beetroot

These sweet and sour beetroot cubes are perfect in a salad of goat's cheese, walnuts and peppery greens. They are great on an antipasto platter or served warmed with lamb.

2 cups wine vinegar
½ cup caster sugar
¾ cup liquid honey (I use viper's bugloss)
1 cup water
12 allspice berries
4 large beetroot, cubed

Sterilise 1 x 1-litre jar or 2 x 500ml jars by washing in hot soapy water, rinsing with boiling water and then keeping hot in the oven at 150°C.

Place the vinegar, sugar, honey, water and allspice berries in a large saucepan and simmer until the sugar has dissolved. Do not stir.

Add the beetroot and simmer uncovered for 20 minutes or until the beetroot is just soft and the liquid is syrupy.

Spoon hot into jars and seal.

Takes 30 minutes
Makes 5 cups

Note: Allspice berries have the combined flavours of cinnamon, clove and nutmeg. They add a lovely warmth to pickles and chutneys.

BEETROOT | *Beetroot requires little care: plant seeds in spring in batches, and continue planting every few weeks right up until the middle of autumn for a constant supply. Pull juvenile plants for baby beets and use the leaves in hearty salads or as pretty garnish. I have even served the stalks as a snack with sea salt for an unusual crudité.*

Passata

Passata is a base to which you can add a hint of this or that to give it a unique flavour. I keep mine simple: garlic and parmesan oil are my favourite additions, or you can use just a simple olive oil. Passata can be preserved in jars or frozen in usable quantities, and once opened it will keep in the fridge for a week.

2kg large juicy tomatoes
4 tablespoons parmesan oil (see note)
2 onions, finely chopped
1 clove garlic, crushed with ½ teaspoon sea salt

Cut a little cross in each of the tomatoes and place in a large bowl. Pour ample boiling water over the tomatoes and leave for 1–2 minutes until you see the skin starting to loosen.

Peel the tomatoes, cut in half and scoop out and discard the seeds.

Heat the parmesan oil in a saucepan and add the onion. Cover and cook gently for at least 10 minutes until the onion is soft and clear but not coloured. Add the garlic and cook for another 2 minutes.

Add the tomato flesh to the softened onion and garlic and cook for 30 minutes. Blend to a smooth sauce. Either seal in sterilised jars or freeze in small batches.

Takes 1 hour
Makes 8 cups

Note: Parmesan oil is a sneaky cheat: the leftover wax rinds from parmesan are thrown into a jar, topped up with oil and left for a month in a cool dark place. I keep a jar permanently in the fridge and keep adding rinds and topping up with oil.

TOMATOES | *Prepare the soil at the end of winter with plenty of well-rotted manure, compost and organic blood and bone, then let it lie fallow while you grow your plants indoors until the cold weather has passed. Plenty of organic matter in the soil will help it to retain the moisture needed to stop tomatoes from splitting due to inconsistent watering.*

Passata

Raspberry & Riesling Jam

2 cups riesling
1½ cups sugar
1kg raspberries, plugs removed

Put the wine in a preserving pan and bring to the boil. Simmer for 10 minutes to reduce by nearly half.

Add half the sugar and allow to dissolve before adding the raspberries with the remaining sugar. Simmer for 10 minutes before testing for setting point by adding a spoonful to a cold saucer and allowing to cool slightly; if it wrinkles when tilted it is ready.

Pour into sterilised dry jars and place a disk of paraffin wax or baking paper directly on the surface. Screw on the lid, or cover with cellophane and a rubber band.

Takes 25 minutes
Makes 2 cups

Raspberry Vinegar

Fantastic in salad dressings, this vinegar will keep for a year. It also makes a great present.

3 cups raspberries, plugs removed
3 cups white vinegar
a few sprigs of thyme

Soak the raspberries in salted water for 5 minutes to remove any bugs. Drain.

Heat the vinegar with the thyme in a large saucepan until nearly boiling.

Drop in the raspberries and allow to cool to room temperature. Stir and pour into a sterilised screw-top jar. Place in a cool dark place for 4–5 days until the colour has come out of the raspberries.

Strain the vinegar through doubled up muslin and discard the fruit and thyme.

Pour into sterilised bottles and seal.

Takes 20 minutes over 4–5 days
Makes 4 cups

RASPBERRIES | *Very easy to grow, raspberries benefit from acid soils – as do blueberries – so growing them together and mulching with pine needles is a good idea. There are both autumn and summer cropping varieties. Prune in autumn by cutting off at ground level any canes that have borne fruit. Thin out the remaining canes, keeping the strongest, and tie them to a fence or stake.*

Raspberry Vinegar

Crab Apple & Blackberry Jelly

Crab apples are not in my home garden but I know a tree that sits neglected on a friend's back lawn. Harvesting them is an annual event that involves calls to verify ripeness and a race to beat the local birds. Naturally high in pectin, crab apples are a useful addition to all jellies, instead of store-bought setting agents.

1kg crab apples
500g blackberries
2 cups plain white sugar

Wash the crab apples and pick over the blackberries and remove stems and leaves. Chop the crab apples roughly.

Place the fruit in a large non-reactive or preserving pan and cover with cold water. Bring to the boil and simmer for 20 minutes. Allow to cool in the pot.

Line a large sieve with muslin and place over a large bowl or bucket to catch the liquid. Empty the cooled contents of the pot into the sieve and tie into a bundle in the muslin. Hang the muslin bundle where it can continue to drain into the bowl. Do not squeeze. Leave to drip through overnight.

Discard the fruit pulp (to the compost!) and return the liquid to the clean pot, with the sugar. Slowly bring to the boil. Boil for 15 minutes until it reaches setting point. Test by putting a drop of liquid on a cold saucer and tilting the saucer: if the liquid wrinkles, it is ready.

Pour into sterilised jars and seal.

Takes 40 minutes over 2 days
Makes 4 cups

Raspberry Leaf & Chamomile Flower Tea

I love the combo of raspberry leaf tea with the calming chamomile.

10 raspberry leaves
3 cups cold water
1 tablespoon dried chamomile flowers
1 teaspoon honey (optional)

Steep the raspberry leaves in cold water in a saucepan for an hour or two before bringing slowly to the boil and simmering for 10 minutes.*

Add the chamomile flowers and steep for a further 3 minutes.

Serve with a spoonful of honey.

Takes about 2 hours
Makes 3 cups

* A little of this liquid cooled and kept aside is soothing on insect bites.

CHAMOMILE | *Chamomile grows easily among herbs and lettuces. Pick the flowers after the dew has dried off, and dry them in the sun.*

autumn

Autumn is abundance; it is the end of crops and glut prices, the season of rich nutty flavours, a source of many leaves, much clearing and raking, and a time of change in the garden. Stakes are pulled out and scrubbed down ready for next spring, berry canes sliced to the ground, mulch spread and bulbs separated and replanted. Gold-tinged reds and row upon row of bottled produce sit in wait to brighten the monotonous winter and the wet spring months. Firewood is stacked, woolly jumpers fluffed up and gumboot socks mended. Autumn is the gentle sashay at the beginning of the long winter dance, where the heat from the sun of summer says its last goodbyes.

an autumn menu

AFTERNOON SUNDOWNER

- Warm Duck & Black Grape Salad
- Nigella-crusted Salmon
- Caramel Chilli Roasted Butternut Pumpkin
- Parmesan-crumbed Aubergine Salad
- Melon & Lime Granita

busy in the autumn garden

TIME TO PLANT

- beetroot
- broad beans
- broccoli
- cabbage
- carrot
- chives
- kale
- leeks
- lettuce (iceberg)
- mustard greens
- oregano
- pak choy
- parsley
- shallots
- silverbeet
- spinach

TIME TO HARVEST

- mushrooms
- nuts
- parsnips
- melons
- capsicum
- cauliflower
- chilli
- persimmon
- pears
- tamarillos
- beetroot
- leeks
- fennel
- figs
- raspberries

TIME TO TEND

- deadhead flowers
- trim off trailing courgette leaves
- cut back this season's fruiting canes
- cut pea vines off at ground level
- burn diseased foliage
- transplant strawberry runners
- rake out straw and add compost
- prune asparagus fern back to ground level

Goat's Cheese, Fig & Honey Beetroot Salad

This hearty salad uses preserves made in the autumn stores section. If you have not made honey beetroot, simply scrub and quarter 2 large beetroot and roast for 25 minutes in a little cold-pressed olive oil until tender.

2 cups pickled honey beetroot cubes (page 110)
4 figs, quartered
½ cup walnut halves
100g soft goat's cheese
1 handful red oak lettuce leaves (or any soft-leaf lettuce)
1 handful rocket leaves
⅓ cup cold-pressed extra virgin olive oil
2 tablespoons red wine vinegar
sea salt

Toss all the ingredients together just before serving.

Takes 5 minutes
Serves 4

FIGS | *Figs start developing on the tree as early as spring and swell all through the summer. The birds wait for them to change from green to deep purple before they swoop in for the lot. It can help to cover a few with plastic bags before the birds beat you to them.*

Warm Duck & Black Grape Salad

1 cooked Peking duck (bought, or see recipe page 155)
1 bunch black grapes, washed and halved
2-3 handfuls rocket leaves
1 bunch coriander
1 large mild red chilli, seeds removed and sliced
1 large spring onion, sliced
¼ cup peanuts, toasted and chopped
1 tablespoon sesame seeds

Dressing
1 tablespoon peanut oil
1 teaspoon sesame oil
1 tablespoon black vinegar
1 tablespoon soy sauce
1 teaspoon crushed fresh ginger root
1 teaspoon palm sugar or brown sugar

Remove the flesh from the duck and, if particularly fatty, render by placing in a 200°C oven for 10 minutes, then remove from the released fat and shred.

Wash and dry the rocket and corriander. Combine with the remaining ingredients and the dressing. Allow the salad to marinate for 10 minutes before serving.

Takes 25 minutes if the duck needs to be rendered; 15 minutes if not
Serves 4-6

Warm Duck & Black Grape Salad

Red Peppers with Goat's Cheese, Lemon & Sage

Red peppers that are long and thin and taper to a point - like the heritage variety Jimmy Nardello or the Anaheim chilli - look and taste fantastic in this recipe.

4 long red chilli peppers
mineral salt and freshly ground pepper
300g chèvre (soft goat's cheese)
zest of 1 lemon
4 tablespoons fresh breadcrumbs
4 teaspoons clear honey (viper's bugloss or borage are both good)
3 tablespoons olive oil
4 sage leaves

Preheat the grill to its highest setting.

Halve the peppers and place them cut-side down on a baking tray. Blacken the skins under the grill then place the peppers in a bowl, covered tightly with plastic wrap to allow the steam to loosen the skins.

Peel away the charred skin from the peppers and discard. Gently wipe the peppers clean, removing the seeds, and season the insides with salt and pepper.

Fill each pepper shell with goat's cheese, add the lemon zest and sprinkle over fresh breadcrumbs. Drizzle the honey over and return briefly to the grill until the top layer of the goat's cheese is caramelised.

Heat the olive oil in a small saucepan and drop in the sage leaves. Fry for 2 minutes before spooning the oil over the filled peppers. Garnish with sage.

Takes 20 minutes
Serves 4

Note: viper's bugloss honey has strong floral, almost rose notes that complement the goat's cheese. If it is unavailable, substitute a thin clear honey with an amber tone rather than a thick or creamy texture.

RED PEPPERS | *Red peppers are easy to grow - even the more exotic varieties. Plant out when the cold has passed at the end of spring. Stake the plants to keep them upright.*

Parmesan-crumbed Aubergine Salad

1 large aubergine
½ cup stoneground flour
2 eggs, beaten
¾ cup finely grated parmesan
¼ cup fresh breadcrumbs
mineral salt and black pepper
¼ cup cold-pressed olive oil
1 bunch rocket leaves
2 large tomatoes, chopped
6-8 black olives
½ red onion, sliced
1 cup fresh basil leaves, torn
⅓ cup smoked paprika aïoli (page 144)

Slice off the stalk end of the aubergine and discard. Slice the aubergine lengthwise into thin slices about 4mm wide.

Coat each slice first in flour, then in egg, then in combined parmesan and breadcrumbs. Season liberally with salt and pepper.

Heat some of the oil in a large frying pan and fry the aubergine slices in batches until golden on both sides. After each batch, wipe out the pan and heat fresh oil.

Arrange the crumbed aubergine slices on plates with the salad ingredients and drizzle everything with the aïoli.

Takes 30 minutes
Serves 4-6

Parmesan-crumbed Aubergine Salad
Overleaf: (left) Caramel Chilli Roasted Butternut
Pumpkin; (right) Braised Shallots

Caramel Chilli Roasted Butternut Pumpkin

1.5kg butternut pumpkin (or use crown pumpkin)
2 tablespoons macadamia oil
4 tablespoons thick dark honey
2 hot chillies, seeds removed and sliced finely
2 teaspoons mineral salt

Preheat the oven to 220°C.

Peel the pumpkin and cut into large chunks. Place in a large bowl.

Combine the oil, honey, chilli and salt and thoroughly coat the pumpkin pieces.

Spread over 2 oven trays with plenty of room for the heat to circulate. Bake for 40 minutes, turning 2 or 3 times, until nice and caramelised.

Takes 1 hour
Serves 4-6

PUMPKIN | *Pumpkins seem to spring up everywhere as the seeds are hardy and often survive the chickens and the composting process. Plant pumpkin seed in spring and watch the plants take off over the lawn towards the sun. They can be trained up a fence, but this makes it difficult for them to support the weight of the crop.*

Braised Shallots

It is satisfying to eat your own stored produce. Summer-cropping shallots are kept in a cool dark place for autumn use.

600-700g shallots, peeled
2 cups vegetable stock
50g butter, cubed
1 stick rosemary
2 bay leaves
1 tablespoon red wine vinegar
1 tablespoon soft dark brown sugar

Preheat the oven to 180°C.

Place all the ingredients in a casserole dish with a lid and bake for 35 minutes.

Remove the lid and continue to cook for a further 15–20 minutes.

Takes 50 minutes
Serves 4-6

SHALLOTS | *Easy to grow, shallots take up less room than onions. The cloves can be poked into the garden among other plants from the end of autumn and throughout winter. When harvesting, save the best-looking cloves to plant again next year.*

Chunky Leek & Potato Soup

2 tablespoons cold-pressed olive oil
100g thick-cut bacon, diced
1 large leek, sliced and washed
1 large floury potato, peeled and diced
3 cups homemade vegetable stock (page 150)
½ cup cream
¼ cup grated parmesan
1-2 teaspoons mineral salt
1 teaspoon white pepper
juice and zest of 1 lemon
1 handful parsley leaves, roughly chopped
2 tablespoons cold-pressed extra virgin
olive oil

Heat the oil in a large saucepan and fry the bacon until nicely browned.

Add the leek and diced potato and sauté until fragrant.

Add the stock and simmer for 20–30 minutes, stirring regularly, until the potato is soft. Remove 2 cups of the soup and reserve. Use a stick blender to purée the remaining soup.

Add the cream, parmesan, salt, pepper and lemon juice, adjusting to suite your taste.

Add the reserved soup back to the saucepan and heat through.

Serve with combined parsley and lemon zest, and a slick of olive oil.

Takes 40 minutes
Serves 6

LEEKS | *It is possible to have leeks in the garden all year round – the crops from early autumn planting will hold through winter – but the most important thing is to get the planting right. Plant them in well-worked soil that has plenty of organic matter worked into it and has good drainage (leeks don't like mud). Before planting, trim them back by half and trim the roots a little, too. Drop the plants into deep holes, deep enough to cover all of the white section of the plant, and water well.*

Cauliflower & Cinnamon Soup

I know this sounds like an odd combination, but I dare you to try it. It is my emergency dinner party fall-back as it takes very little time, is extra cheap to make and it tastes exotic.

50g butter
1 large onion, diced
1 cinnamon stick
½ teaspoon toasted cumin seeds, crushed
1 large head of cauliflower, leaves removed
4 cups vegetable stock
½ cup cream
mineral salt and white pepper to taste

Melt the butter and add the onion, cinnamon and cumin. Cover with a lid and cook gently for 10 minutes.

Prepare the cauliflower by snapping off the curds or florets. Keep the stalk whole and add to the pot with the curds and the stock. Simmer for about 15 minutes until the cauliflower curds are tender. Discard the stalk and the cinnamon stick.

Blend in the cream, tasting and adjusting the seasoning as you go.

Takes 25 minutes
Serves 4-6

CAULIFLOWER | *Rich clay-based soils are best for cauliflower and it needs a lot of space. Experts say to bend the side leaves over the top of the cauliflower to keep it white. I cover it with a big cabbage leaf so I can easily peer under and check for bugs; the bonus is that I can paint the outside of the cabbage leaf with neem oil or pyrethrum to deter bugs.*

Rosemary Lamb & Aubergine Casserole

1kg lamb shoulder, diced
¼ cup stoneground flour
2 teaspoons mineral salt and 1 teaspoon ground black pepper
2-3 tablespoons cold-pressed peanut oil
1 onion, finely chopped
1 carrot, diced
1 whole lemon cut into 6 wedges
1 big stick rosemary
12 black olives
1 large aubergine, cut into chunks
½ cup parsley, roughly chopped

Preheat the oven to 180°C.

Toss the diced lamb in the combined flour, salt and pepper.

Heat the oil in a casserole dish and cook the lamb in batches until brown. Add the onion, carrot, lemon wedges, rosemary and olives. Cover and place in the oven for 1 hour.

Remove from the oven, add the aubergine and stir. Cover and return to the oven for another 25 minutes. Fold through chopped parsley before serving.

Takes 1 hour 35 minutes
Serves 4-6

Roasted Venison Backstraps with Baby Beets

Resting the venison is the key to this recipe. The general rule for resting meat is to rest for half of the cooking time; however, with venison, resting it for as long as it was cooked gives a tender and succulent result.

1kg venison backstraps
1 teaspoon freshly ground black pepper
12 baby beetroot, scrubbed
1 teaspoon salt
3 tablespoons peanut oil
1 teaspoon salt, extra
¼ cup water reserved from blanching the beetroot
2 tablespoons kecap manis (thick, sweet soy sauce)

Wash and dry the venison and sprinkle with pepper. Allow it to come to room temperature.

Place the beetroot in a saucepan and cover with cold water. Cover and bring to the boil, then add the salt. Cook at a gentle boil until just tender, 5–10 minutes depending on the size of the beets. Reserve ¼ cup of cooking water before draining.

Heat the peanut oil in a heavy-based frying pan and sprinkle with salt. Add the venison and cook on one side for 3–5 minutes until blood begins to bead on the surface. Turn and watch closely for the blood to rise again. Roll to sear the edges. Place the venison on a plate in a warm place and cover with baking paper and a teatowel.

Add the reserved water and kecap manis to the pan and use a wooden spoon to scratch up the pan scrapings and combine them in the sauce. Add the beetroot and simmer for 1–2 minutes before serving with the thickly sliced venison and sauce.

Takes 35 minutes
Serves 4

Note: When frying meat, if you are making a jus or gravy from the pan scrapings do not use a non-stick pan as this prevents the meat browning from building up on the pan's surface.

Roasted Venison Backstraps with Baby Beets

Twice-cooked Pressed Belly of Free-range Pork

This recipe needs to be started 2 days in advance – it is for the mad perfectionist. It took me a week of working in the late late evenings after my restaurant shift to figure this one out, and is a pleasure to pass it on to the lover of cooking. I am loath to admit that the pressing can be left out: its only purpose is to create a satisfyingly (to the perfectionist) uniform end result.

500g non-iodised salt
3 litres water
3 or 4 bay leaves
2kg free-range farmed belly of pork, boneless (ask the butcher to score it for you)
1 onion, roughly chopped
1 carrot, roughly chopped
3 sticks celery, roughly chopped
2 cups water
weights (I use my biggest cookbooks)
2 tablespoons tamari or soy sauce
2 teaspoons honey
2 tablespoons peanut oil

Place the salt, water and bay leaves in a large container, and stir to dissolve the salt. Wash and dry the pork and add to the water. Place in the fridge and leave for 12 hours. Remove the pork, rinse and pat dry.

Preheat the oven to 160°C.

Place the onion, carrot and celery in a deep roasting dish and add the 2 cups of water. Put an ovenproof rack on top so that it doesn't touch the water (I use a cake rack). Place the pork on top of the rack and cover with baking paper and then cover the whole pan with foil.

Cook for 1½ hours. Remove from the oven and allow to cool.

Leaving the baking paper in place, sandwich the pork between 2 baking sheets or flat trays. Transfer to the fridge and place heavy weights on the top tray. Leave for another 12 hours.

Remove the weights and peel off the paper.

It is easier to cut the pork now before the crackled crust is formed, but there is a sacrifice in moistness with the second cooking if cut now. I prefer to wait and then use an electric bread knife to cut through the crackling when serving.

Heat the grill to a medium-high setting. Place the pork under the grill for 10 minutes until the top is starting to bubble and pop. Remove and brush with the combined tamari, honey and peanut oil before returning to the grill for another 5–10 minutes (watch carefully, as the sugar in the sweet soy can quickly go past black to actually burnt).

Takes 2½ hours over 3 days
Serves 8

Twice-cooked Pressed Belly of Free-range Pork

Oven-baked Snapper Parcels with Leek & Florence Fennel

Exceptionally juicy, this recipe is particularly good with a larger fillet of snapper, served with brown rice and wilted spinach.

1 small leek
1 large bulb Florence fennel, finely sliced
2 tablespoons lemon juice
1 teaspoon salt
2 tablespoons water
25g butter
600g snapper fillet, skinless, cut into 3cm chunks

Slice the leeks into rings and soak in water to remove the dirt, lift out and drain well. Combine with the fennel, lemon juice, salt and water.

Melt the butter in a saucepan and add the leek and fennel mixture. Cook until wilted and soft but not coloured. Allow to cool.

Preheat the oven to 200°C.

Tear off 4 large rectangles of baking paper or foil and fold over into squares. Divide the fennel mixture and fish between the squares and fold the edges of the squares together, crimping and folding to seal. Place the parcels in a roasting dish.

Bake in the oven for 10 minutes. Remove the parcels from the oven and allow to rest for 5 minutes before serving.

Takes 25 minutes
Serves 4

Angel Hair Spaghetti with Garlic & Chilli

The simplest supper is often the best. This recipe is super-fast and satisfying; even the salt takes on a lovely caramelised flavour.

400-500g homemade pasta, cut on the finest setting
¼ cup cold-pressed olive oil
4 fresh chillies, diced
4 cloves garlic, sliced
1 teaspoon sea salt

Cook the pasta in boiling salted water for 4 minutes. Drain.

Meanwhile, heat the oil in the pan and add the chillies. Cook for 2 minutes before adding the garlic and the salt. Cook for another 2 minutes or until the garlic is just starting to turn brown. Remove from the heat and toss through the spaghetti.

Takes 4 minutes
Serves 4

Angel Hair Spaghetti with Garlic & Chilli

Nigella-crusted Salmon

If you are a pepper lover who has a tendency to overdo the pepper, nigella may be about to become your best friend. It has the flavour of pepper without all the heat, so keeping a little toasted and crushed on hand may help tone down some previously less fortunate dishes.

½ cup nigella seeds
1 tablespoon sea salt
4 x 150g pieces of salmon fillet, skinless
1 tablespoon sunflower oil
1 teaspoon red wine vinegar
1 teaspoon horseradish

Preheat the grill to 200°C.

Crush the nigella seeds lightly with the salt, using either a pestle and mortar or a rolling pin.

Combine the oil, vinegar and horseradish. Brush the salmon on both sides with this mixture. Press the skin side of the salmon fillets into the nigella and salt.

Grill for 3–4 minutes on each side before serving.

Serve with roasted tomatoes and preserved lemon (page 42).

Takes 15 minutes
Serves 4

NIGELLA SEEDS/BLACK CUMIN

Nigella is a member of the buttercup family. It makes an excellent bee-attracting companion plant and a pretty groundcover. Harvest quickly once the seed has set and hang upside down in paper bags to catch the falling seeds. Don't plant near legumes as it is said to inhibit their growth.

Chicken & Juniper Pies

200g rough puff pastry (page 152)
100g thick-cut smoked bacon, diced
1 small onion, sliced
4 juniper berries, crushed
1 teaspoon mineral salt and ½ teaspoon white pepper
2 tablespoons butter
2 tablespoons flour
1 cup whole milk
500g boneless chicken thighs, diced
2 egg yolks

Preheat the oven to 180°C.

Grease 4 large deep ramekins or ovenproof dishes. Roll out the pastry and cut 4 rounds for the tops of the pies. Chill the pastry rounds until ready to put in the oven.

Brown the bacon in a large frying pan. Remove from the pan.

Add the onion, juniper berries, salt and pepper to the pan and cook gently in the fat from the bacon for 20 minutes. Add a little butter if required. Remove and set aside.

Melt the butter in the same pan and add the flour. Cook for 1–2 minutes. Remove the pan from the heat and add the milk. Return to the heat and stir constantly until very thick.

Combine the diced chicken, bacon, onion, white sauce and 1 egg yolk. Spoon the mixture into the prepared ramekins and cover each dish with a pastry top. Brush the pastry with the remaining egg yolk, then cut a small hole in the centre of each top to allow steam to escape. Bake for 25–30 minutes.

Takes 1 hour
Serves 4

Note: If using store-bought pastry, choose one made with butter and no extra additives.

Nigella-crusted Salmon

Melon & Lime Granita

Timing is all for this recipe – you need to keep the melon ready until the first limes appear. Getting the sweetness right for a melon sorbet can be a delicate balancing act: too little and the sorbet tastes like cucumber (lovely with chilled prawns); too much and it becomes sickly. Limes are the perfect partner for this.

350g sugar
350 ml water
3 tablespoons lime juice
1 honeydew melon, peeled, deseeded and chopped (approx 1kg flesh)

Place the sugar and water in a saucepan over a low heat to dissolve, then simmer gently without stirring for 20 minutes. Cool.

When sugar syrup is cool, add with the lime juice to the chopped melon and blend in a food processor until smooth.

Place in a shallow container with a tight-fitting lid in the freezer. After 3 hours give it a good rake-up with a large fork, then place back in the freezer. Continue raking with a fork regularly until a lovely smooth ice is formed. Alternatively process using an ice-cream machine as directed for sorbets and ices.

Takes 25 minutes, plus chilling time
Makes 2 litres

MELONS | *Melons need to be planted in early summer to make the most of the growing season. They like to climb, which means their heavy fruit often needs to be supported. A simple sling made out of pantyhose is good for this.*

Baked Persimmons

4 large firm fuyu (non-astringent) persimmons
4 small cubes of butter
4 tablespoons vino cotto
¼ cup mascarpone
1 tablespoon honey
2 amaretti biscuits, crushed

Preheat the oven to 180°C.

Remove the top leaves of the persimmons using a sharp knife and make a conical hole. Place the persimmons in an ovenproof dish. Put a cube of butter in each hole and top up with 1 tablespoon of vino cotto.

Bake for 20 minutes.

Serve with the combined mascarpone and honey, crushed biscuits and an extra slick of vino cotto.

Takes 25 minutes
Serves 4

Melon & Lime Granita

Passionfruit Ice Cream

The sweet and tart of passionfruit is perfect with any creamy dessert. The ice cream requires at least 4 hours' freezing time, so it is best to make it the night before.

250g passionfruit pulp (including pips)
zest and juice of 1 orange
300g caster sugar
200ml water
3 egg whites
300ml cream

Combine the passionfruit pulp and the orange juice and zest.

Place the sugar and water in a pan and bring to the boil. Boil for 6–7 minutes until it thickens slightly (120°C on a sugar thermometer).

Use an electric beater to whisk the egg whites in a large bowl. When the whites are fluffy, slowly pour in the hot syrup and keep beating until the meringue mix is firm and thick.

In a separate bowl, whisk the cream until thick but still soft, as it is easier to fold together if it's not as thick as the meringue mixture. Fold the two mixtures together, then loosely fold in the passionfruit pulp.

Pour into a deep baking pan and place in the freezer for at least 4 hours, until firm.

Takes 25 minutes, plus chilling time
Makes 2 litres

PASSIONFRUIT | *Passionfruit vines crop successfully for around 5-7 years. Prune back hard after autumn fruiting is completed. Keep well watered in the spring and summer, as this is when they are putting all their energy into setting and growing fruit.*

Pear & Rosemary Eve's Puddings

120g butter
4 small sprigs fresh rosemary
¾ cup sugar
2 eggs
¾ cup flour
1 teaspoon baking powder
1 teaspoon ground ginger
2 pears, peeled, cored and halved

Preheat the oven to 160°C.

Lightly fry the rosemary in a little of the butter in a medium saucepan, then remove from the heat and add the remaining butter. Leave to melt and cool slightly.

Beat together the sugar and eggs, using an electric beater until really light and fluffy, or hand-whisk for at least 5 minutes.

Remove the rosemary from the butter and set aside. Add the melted butter, flour, baking powder and ginger to the egg and sugar mixture. Fold together quickly to form a batter.

Divide the batter between four greased ramekins or individual ovenproof dishes. Add a pear half to each dish, with a sprig of the wilted rosemary.

Bake for 30 minutes until the sponge springs back to the touch.

Takes 40 minutes
Serves 4

Passionfruit Ice Cream
Overleaf: (left) Pears Poached in Rhubarb
& Allspice Syrup; (right) Honey Apple Fritters

Pears Poached in Rhubarb & Allspice Syrup

3 cups sugar

4 cups water

6 stems rhubarb, chopped

6 allspice berries, crushed

1 vanilla pod, split in half and seeds scraped out and reserved

4 pears, peeled

Place the sugar in a deep saucepan and add the water. Slowly bring to the boil, allowing the sugar to melt. Do not stir.

Gently lower the rhubarb into the sugar syrup with the allspice, vanilla pod and seeds. Simmer for 5 minutes before adding the pears.

Slice the bottom off each pear so it will sit upright when served. Add the pears to the syrup and simmer for 15 minutes until tender. Serve with a ladle of the spiced rhubarb syrup.

Takes 25 minutes
Serves 4

Note: The remaining rhubarb syrup makes a refreshing pink cordial when served with soda and a squeeze of lime.

PEARS | *For a birthday I was given a pear tree in a large pot. It has made six house moves, survived dire neglect at one point and the occasional holiday-induced drought. However, it doggedly puts out the loveliest flowers each year and bears fruit like a trooper. It is a reminder that a life well lived (with a few good challenges) also bears fruit.*

Honey Apple Fritters

2 large apples, peeled, cored, halved and sliced

lemon juice

50g butter, melted

1 tablespoon thick dark honey

100g stoneground organic flour

1 pinch mineral salt

½ cup milk

1 teaspoon lemon juice

2 eggs, separated

Prepare the apples and drop into a bowl of water and lemon juice to prevent them from discolouring while you make the batter.

Melt together the butter and honey and set aside to cool.

Sift the flour and salt into a large bowl and make a well in the middle.

Add the milk, lemon juice, egg yolks and melted butter and honey into the well and loosely incorporate the flour.

Whisk the egg whites until fluffy and fold through the batter. Fold in the sliced apple.

Panfry spoonfuls of the batter on a medium heat with a little melted butter for 3–4 minutes on each side.

Takes 25 minutes
Serves 4-6

Smoked Paprika Aïoli

2 egg yolks at room temperature
1 teaspoon Dijon-style mustard
1 teaspoon sweet smoked paprika
3 cloves garlic, crushed
1 pinch salt
1 pinch white pepper
300ml canola oil
1 tablespoon boiling water
½ teaspoon red wine vinegar
1 pinch cayenne or hot chilli powder

In a medium-sized bowl beat together the egg yolks, mustard, paprika, garlic, salt and pepper.

Place the oil in a jug and very slowly drip it into the egg yolk mixture while whisking furiously. Whisk in the boiling water and the red wine vinegar.

Taste and add cayenne or chilli powder to taste.

Takes 10 minutes
Makes 2 cups of aïoli.

Dried Chilli Flakes

25-30 homegrown chillies
white vinegar

Harvest the chillies and, wearing rubber gloves, wash them in a bowl of warm water and vinegar.

Dry the chillies thoroughly and cut in half from tip to stem, exposing the seeds. Remove most of the seeds and discard.

Spread cut side up on wire racks and place in the sun to dry, turning periodically.

Alternatively, place the chilli halves on wire racks and cook in an oven at 80°C for 3–4 hours, turning periodically until dry.

Wearing dry rubber gloves, crumble the chillies onto a large sheet of paper, then roll the paper into a funnel to transfer the chilli flakes to storage jars. Store in a cool dark place.

Takes 3-4 hours
Makes 1 small jar

Pickled Onions

It is remarkably easy to prepare your own jars of pickled onions. The chilli really does permeate the onion, so if you don't like it hot, leave it out. Pickled onions make a gutsy addition to an aged cheddar cheeseboard.

200g salt
2 litres water
2kg pickling onions, peeled
1.5 litres white wine vinegar
1 tablespoon coriander seeds
8 cardamom pods
6 cloves
3 bay leaves
2 large or 4 small chillies
¾ cup sugar

Dissolve the salt in the water in a large saucepan over high heat. Cool completely before adding the peeled onions to the brine (otherwise the onions will go wrinkly). Weigh the onions down with a small plate or saucer and leave overnight (12 hours).

Prepare 2 x 1-litre jars by washing with hot soapy water and then placing in a cold oven and bringing up to 150°C. Keep the jars in the oven until ready to fill.

Prepare the pickling liquor by combining the remaining ingredients in a large saucepan and boiling for 5 minutes. Cool completely.

Remove the onions from the brine and rinse thoroughly. Pack them into the prepared jars. Pour over the pickling liquor, dividing the spices as evenly as possible (I find it easiest to collect them in a tea strainer and then redistribute between the jars).

Seal and leave for at least 2 weeks before eating.

Takes 30 minutes over 2 days
Makes 3 x 1 litre jars

Dried Chilli Flakes
Overleaf: (right) Plum Anise Sauce

Plum Anise Sauce

2kg dark plums
1 cup vinegar
1 cup brown sugar
3 star anise, roughly crushed
4 whole cloves
3 allspice berries, crushed

Cut a cross in the base of each plum and put in a large bowl. Cover the plums with boiling water and leave for 1 minute until the skin begins to loosen. Peel, then halve the plums and remove the stones.

Chop the plum flesh roughly and add it to a large saucepan with the vinegar and brown sugar. Tie the spices loosely in a large piece of muslin, add to the pan and bring all to the boil. Simmer for 30 minutes. Turn off and leave to cool completely on the stove.

Remove the spices and blend the plum mixture until smooth. Pour into sterilised bottles and seal.

Takes about 1 hour
Makes 4 cups

Fennel Seed & Sage Tisane

1 teaspoon fennel seeds, bruised
6-8 sage leaves
1 teaspoon honey
2 cups of boiling water

Place the fennel seeds and sage leaves in a teapot and add boiling water. Steep for 5 minutes before serving with honey.

Takes 6 minutes
Makes 2 cups

Orange Chilli Cheese

This recipe is similar to a quince paste or a fruit cheese, hence the name. I like to set it in small discs that can be added to antipasti or cheese platters. It has a good kick and is purely for lovers of heat.

1.5kg orange chillies, deseeded
1kg oranges
1 litre water
sugar
1 large piece of muslin

Place the chillies in a preserving pan.

Remove the zest from the oranges using a potato peeler, being careful not to leave any white pith on the zest. Alternatively, use a zester.

Remove the pith from the oranges using a sharp paring knife and discard. Roughly chop the orange flesh before adding it to the pan.

Add the water and boil for 1 hour.

Place a large sieve over a large bowl, line it with a large piece of muslin and pour the orange and chilli mixture through, straining out the pulp. Tie the muslin into a bundle and suspend it over the bowl to catch the liquid; or alternatively, leave the bundle to rest in the sieve over the bowl. Leave overnight.

Discard the pulp. Pour the liquid into a measuring jug and weigh. Return the liquid to the preserving pan and add half the weight of sugar. For example, if the weight of the liquid is 800g, add 400g of sugar.

Boil, stirring regularly, until thick. The desired temperature is between 106°C and 108°C on a sugar thermometer; this should take around 20 minutes.

Pour into lightly greased mini-muffin pans, filling each by only one third to create small disks. Alternatively, pour into a greaseproof slice pan (30cm x 20cm) and allow to set, then cut into small squares and wrap in wax paper. Store in an airtight container in the pantry until required.

Takes 1½ hours over 2 days
Makes 20 small squares

Orange Chilli Cheese

homemade staples

Vegetable Stock

Vegetable stock takes a little bit of time, but it's worth it. It is excellent for adding a little flavour to cooked vegetables; and it's essential in risotto. Onion, carrot and celery form the basis of any vegetable stock. Other vegetables may be added, but be aware that they will affect the flavour.

1 leek
1 onion
2 carrots
3 sticks celery
1 bay leaf
4 peppercorns
1 bunch parsley, stalks only
4 ½ cups of water

Place all the ingredients in a large pot and bring to the boil.

Reduce to a simmer and simmer for up to 30 minutes.

Strain. Return the stock to a clean pan and continue to simmer and reduce until the stock has a good flavour and is a storable quantity.

Takes 30 minutes, plus reducing time
Makes 4 cups

Note: It is important that salt is not added to stock; it is better to salt the dish the stock is used in after tasting it.

Spice Oil

A perfect finish for a simple dish of steamed vegetables. Spice oil is also particularly good tossed with cauliflower and then roasted, or drizzled over a homemade dahl.

½ cup cold-pressed organic olive oil
1 tablespoon ground turmeric
2 tablespoons fennel seeds, lightly crushed
1 tablespoon coriander seeds, lightly crushed
2 teaspoons cumin seeds, lightly crushed
1 teaspoon rock salt

Heat the oil in a small pan and add the spices.

Fry until fragrant and the seeds begin to pop. Remove from the heat and either use while hot or allow to cool before storing in an airtight glass jar.

Takes 2 minutes
Makes ½ cup

Caesar Salad Dressing

2 egg yolks at room temperature
1 teaspoon Dijon mustard
1 clove garlic, crushed
2 anchovies and 1 teaspoon anchovy oil
1 pinch white pepper
300ml canola oil
1 tablespoon boiling water
½ teaspoon red wine vinegar

In a medium-sized bowl, beat together the egg yolks, mustard, garlic, anchovies, anchovy oil and pepper.

Place the canola oil in a jug and very slowly drip into the yolk mix while whisking furiously. Whisk in the boiling water and the red wine vinegar.

Takes 5 minutes
Makes 2 cups

Blind Baking

Preheat the oven to 190°C.

Grease and line a tart dish with pastry. Chill for 20 minutes, until firm.

Line the pastry shell with crumpled baking paper and dried beans or rice.

Bake for 15 minutes or until a pale biscuit colour.

Remove the baking paper and beans.

Brush the pastry with egg white to seal, and pop back in the oven for 5 minutes.

Rough Puff Pastry

Homemade pastry with organic flour and butter is like a different species to the stuff bought in shops. It does take a little time but leaves immense satisfaction on the palate and barely a crumb on the plate.

300g plain flour, chilled
200g unsalted butter, chilled and cubed
1 generous pinch mineral salt
¾ cup iced water
extra flour for rolling

Sift the flour into a chilled bowl (pop it in the freezer for 10 minutes).

Add the cubed butter and salt to the flour and, using a table knife, add enough of the iced water to form a lightly bound dough. Knead briefly and gently with one hand.

Wrap the pastry in waxed paper and chill for 10 minutes in the fridge.

On a floured benchtop, carefully roll out the pastry into a rectangle, fold it into 3 (a bit like a letter), then roll again until it is back to the original rectangle size. Fold into 3 again and chill for another 10 minutes.

Repeat the folding and rolling twice more, or until the butter is barely visible.

Chill again before rolling out and cutting for the specific recipe.

Takes about 30 minutes
Makes 400g

Note: *If freezing the pastry, roll into sheets and separate the sheets with waxed paper.*

Caraway Pastry

¼ cup cold water
1⅓ cups organic plain flour
1 pinch salt
1 teaspoon caraway seeds, toasted and crushed
180g cold butter

Measure the cold water and keep nearby.

Sift the flour into a pile on a clean benchtop or into a large bowl, and add the salt and caraway seeds.

Grate the butter and quickly rub it into the flour using your fingertips, to the consistency of rough breadcrumbs. Make a well in the middle.

Tip the cold water into the well and, using a spoon, draw the flour mixture into the well until the water is soaked up.

Use the heel of your hand to smear the mix away from you, then draw it back into the pile and smear it away again to combine.

Shape into a ball, dust with a bit more flour and leave in the fridge for half an hour to relax.

Takes 10 minutes, plus relaxing time
Makes enough pastry to line a fluted tart dish up to 24cm diameter

Fast Rich Sweet Shortcrust Pastry

180g stoneground plain flour
1 pinch salt
100g unsalted butter, softened
3 egg yolks
100g icing sugar
½ teaspoon vanilla extract
extra flour for rolling

Sift the flour and salt onto a clean benchtop or into a large bowl and make a well in the middle.

Add the softened butter, egg yolks, icing sugar and vanilla extract and use a palate knife to stir them together in the well. Sweep the circle of the palate knife wider to incorporate the flour from around the edges.

When the dough has come together, knead briefly and then chill for 20 minutes.

Roll the pastry out to the required shape on a floured benchtop.

Takes 10 minutes, plus relaxing time
Makes enough pastry to line a fluted tart dish up to 24cm diameter

Note: This pastry can be made very quickly in a food processor, but because the blade will incorporate tiny air bubbles it will not be quite as crisp. Simply place all the ingredients in the bowl with the standard cutting blade and pulse to bring together.

Plain Pasta for Pappardelle, Fettuccine or Angel Hair Pasta

Tipo 'oo' is a fine grade wheat flour that is lovely and soft. It has a high gluten content, which is how it bonds to form the pasta dough. It is possible to make pasta with a plain flour, but for best results buy tipo oo and store it in the fridge for all pasta-making forays.

200g tipo oo flour (or white stoneground flour)
2 whole eggs
2 tablespoons vegetable stock or water
1 tablespoon cold-pressed organic olive oil
1 pinch freshly grated nutmeg (optional)
1 pinch salt
¼ cup flour extra for kneading and rolling

Make a pile of flour on a clean benchtop or use a large bowl. Use your fist to form a large well in the centre and add all remaining ingredients into the well.

With a table knife use a stirring motion to incorporate the liquids into the flour until a sticky dough is formed.

Knead until the dough is firm and smooth, and bounces back when pressed. Leave to rest for 10 minutes.

Cut the dough into 4 and knead each quarter briefly before rolling through a pasta machine from the widest setting to the narrowest setting.

Prepare a clean tray dusted with flour for the cut pasta. Cut each segment as required: use the wider cutter for fettuccine and the narrow cutter for angel hair pasta. Cut pappardelle by hand into 1.5–2cm wide strips.

Takes 20 minutes
Serves 4

Note: Fresh pasta freezes well and cooks well from frozen; it will require a few more minutes of cooking time. Allow to dry before freezing in portions.

Wholemeal Lasagne Sheets

Rather than using wholemeal flour, the best result comes from adding wheat bran to tipo oo flour.

150g tipo oo flour (or stoneground flour)
25g wheat bran
25g ground almonds
2 whole eggs, lightly beaten
2 tablespoons or waterns vegetable stock or water
1 tablespoon cold-pressed organic olive oil
1 pinch freshly grated nutmeg (optional)
1 pinch salt
½ cup flour extra for kneading and rolling

Make a pile with the flour, wheat bran and almond meal on a clean benchtop (or use a bowl if you prefer). Use your fist to form a large well in the centre and add all the remaining ingredients into the well.

With a table knife, use a stirring motion to incorporate the ingredients into the flour until a sticky dough is formed.

Knead until the dough is firm and smooth, and bounces back when pressed. Leave to rest for at least 10 minutes but preferably 30 minutes.

Cut the dough into 4 and knead briefly before rolling each quarter through a pasta machine from the widest setting to the narrowest setting.

Prepare a clean tray dusted with flour for the rolled pasta. Cut each strip into 20cm lengths to fit your lasagne dish.

Takes 20 minutes
Makes 2 x 20cm lasagne dishes

Olive Oil Bread

2 tablespoons (25g) dried yeast
1 tablespoon honey
1 cup warm water (not boiling, just warmer than lukewarm)
400g plain flour
1 teaspoon mineral salt
2 tablespoons olive oil
olive oil, rosemary, sea salt, olives for topping

Dissolve the yeast and honey in the warm water.

Sift the flour well and add the salt before making a well in the centre.

Pour in the dissolved yeast mixture and the olive oil.

Mix together to form a dough. Knead by gathering the dough together and then pushing it away. This needs to be done for about 10 minutes.

Leave in a warm place to rise until it is silky and puffy.

Oil 1 or 2 baking sheets and dust a rolling pin with flour. Roll the dough into 1 large or 2 small ovals, brush with olive oil and sprinkle over any toppings and cover. Leave until doubled in size.

Preheat the oven to 200°C.

Bake the loaf/loaves for about 20 minutes, depending on size. Test for doneness by lifting a loaf with a cloth and tapping the bottom. If it sounds hollow it is ready.

Takes 2 hours
Makes 1 large loaf or 2 small loaves

Note: Keep the flour on hand – you may need a little more to strengthen the dough, and you will need it for rolling out.

Peking Duck

If you are unable to buy a prepared Peking duck, here is a simple way of making one at home. Use it to make the Warm Duck & Black Grape Salad (page 120).

2kg free-range farmed duck
2 tablespoons maltose
1 tablespoon thick dark honey
2 tablespoons boiling water

Bring a very large pot of water to the boil. Plunge the duck in the boiling water and leave for 3–4 minutes.

Remove the duck, drain the water from the cavity and gently pat dry.

Combine the maltose and honey with 2 tablespoons of fresh boiling water. Brush this mixture all over the duck then leave uncovered in the fridge for 6 hours or overnight.

Preheat the oven to 200°C. Roast the duck for 1½ hours, turning if necessary to promote even browning. If the bird is browning too fast, cover with foil for the last ½ hour.

Allow to rest for 10 minutes before cutting into rough chunks to serve. If using for the warm duck and black grape salad, allow the duck to cool completely before removing and shredding the flesh.

Takes 8 hours (including 6 hours resting)
Serves 4

Note: Rubbing the inside of the duck with a paste made from five-spice and soy sauce adds a lovely perfumed flavour.

glossary & conversions

Demerara sugar
Raw brown sugar that takes its colour from a light treatment of molasses.

Five-spice
A Chinese spice mixture made from equal parts of anise pepper, star anise, cassia or cinnamon, cloves and fennel seed.

Grana Padano Cheese
This hard Italian cheese has similar qualities to Parmesan, but it is generally found to be more affordable.

Gravlax
A Nordic specialty of salmon that has been cold cured with salt, sugar and herbs. It is traditionally served in thin slices with dark grain bread.

Kale
This dark-green, smooth and curly, leaved vegetable can be substituted for cooked cabbage in any recipe. It's not eaten raw due to its tough fibrous texture.

Medjool dates
These large dates have a wrinkled skin and a fudge-like texture. They should be plump and shiny and are usually found in the chiller of the fruit and vegetable section of the supermarket.

Passata
A smooth versatile tomato sauce that is relatively unembellished by herbs and spices.

Pecorino Cheese
A pungent and salty cheese made from sheeps milk. Pecorino is an Italian cheese from the same group as Parmesan.

Snow peas/mangetout
The pods of the snow pea are flat. In French, Mangetout translates to 'eat all', thus this variety of pea is eaten pod and all while it is still unripe.

Stoneground flour
Slightly heavier than plain flour, this whole-wheat flour is ground between rotating stones. The use of whole wheat means that the wheat germ and bran are included in the flour.

Tahini or tahina
Tahini is a paste made from toasted sesame seeds and is commonly used in the well-known dip hummus.

Tisane
Tisanes or herbal teas are caffeine free and made from herbs, spices, roots and flowers that are edible and free from sprays.

Vino Cotto
Vino cotto is a sweet Italian 'cooked wine' syrup made from grape must and juice that has been reduced then aged in oak barrels.

The following amounts have been rounded up or down for convenience. All have been kitchen-tested.

ABBREVIATIONS

g	gram
kg	kilogram
mm	millimetre
cm	centimetre
ml	millilitre
°C	degrees Celsius

CAKE TIN SIZES

METRIC	IMPERIAL/US
15cm	6 inches
18cm	7 inches
20cm	8 inches
23cm	9 inches
25cm	10 inches
28cm	11 inches

WEIGHT CONVERSIONS

METRIC	IMPERIAL/US
25g	1 oz
50g	2 oz
75g	3 oz
100g	3½ oz
125g	4½ oz
150g	5 oz
175g	6 oz
200g	7 oz
225g	8 oz
250g	9 oz
275g	9½ oz
300g	10½ oz
325g	11½ oz
350g	12½ oz
375g	13 oz
400g	14 oz
450g	16 oz (1 lb)
500g	17½ oz
750g	26½ oz
1kg	35 oz (2¼ lb)

TEMPERATURE CONVERSIONS

Celsius	Fahrenheit	Gas
100°C	225°F	¼
125°C	250°F	½
150°C	300°F	2
160°C	325°F	3
170°C	325°F	3
180°C	350°F	4
190°C	375°F	5
200°C	400°F	6
210°C	425°F	7
220°C	425°F	7
230°C	450°F	8
250°C	500°F	9

LENGTH CONVERSIONS

METRIC	IMPERIAL/US
0.5cm	¼ inch
1cm	½ inch
2.5cm	1 inch
5cm	2 inches
10cm	4 inches
20cm	8 inches
30cm	12 inches (1 foot)

LIQUID CONVERSIONS

METRIC	IMPERIAL	CUP MEASURES
5ml (1 tsp)	¼ fl oz	1 tsp
15ml (1 tbsp)	½ fl oz	1 tbsp
30ml (⅛ cup)	1 fl oz	⅛ cup
60ml (¼ cup)	2 fl oz	¼ cup
125ml (½ cup)	4 fl oz	½ cup
150ml	5 fl oz (¼ pint)	⅔ cup
175ml	6 fl oz	¾ cup
250ml (1 cup)	8 fl oz	1 cup
300ml	10 fl oz (½ pint)	1¼ cups
375ml	12 fl oz	1½ cups
500ml (2 cups)	16 fl oz	2 cups
600ml	20 fl oz (1 pint)	2½ cups

NOTE: The Australian metric tablespoon measures 20ml.

index

ACKNOWLEDGEMENTS |

I would like to thank some of the many supporters and tasters who have taken part in this book: Michael Gifkins, Belinda Cooke, Kieran Scott, Lauraine Jacobs, Kathy Paterson, Heather Tate, my parents and my brothers, my husband Jonathan Tuohey and his family. Also David Chaloner, Briar McCormack, Juliet Perano, Clinton Squibb, Louise Moulin, Jessica Bartlett, Patricia Colemore Williams and Karen Hall, and our ever-enduring landlords Campbell and Dionne.

First published in 2011 by New Holland Publishers (NZ) Ltd
Auckland • Sydney • London • Cape Town

www.newhollandpublishers.co.nz

218 Lake Road, Northcote, Auckland 0627, New Zealand
Unit 1, 66 Gibbes Street, Chatswood, NSW 2067, Australia
86–88 Edgware Road, London W2 2EA, United Kingdom
80 McKenzie Street, Cape Town 8001, South Africa

ISBN: 978 1 86966 316 2

Publishing manager: Christine Thomson
Editor: Gillian Tewsley
Design: Athena Sommerfield
Front cover: (top left) Broad Bean and Prawn Pasta with Sorrel; (bottom right) Pears Poached in Rhubarb and Allspice Syrup.

A catalogue record for this book is available from
the National Library of New Zealand.

10 9 8 7 6 5 4 3 2 1

Colour reproduction and printing by Craft Print International Ltd, Singapore.